Fall 2000
HP-101

Reflections from the North Country

The Fesler-Lampert *Minnesota Heritage Book* Series

This series is published with the generous assistance of the John K. and Elsie Lampert Fesler Fund and David R. and Elizabeth P. Fesler. Its mission is to republish significant out-of-print books that contribute to our understanding and appreciation of Minnesota and the Upper Midwest.

SIGURD F. OLSON

Reflections from the North Country

ILLUSTRATED BY LESLIE KOUBA

University of Minnesota Press
MINNEAPOLIS

First published in hardcover in the United States by
Alfred A. Knopf, Inc., New York, and simultaneously in Canada
by Random House of Canada Limited, Toronto.
First University of Minnesota Press edition, 1998. Reprinted
by arrangement with Alfred A. Knopf, Inc.

Grateful acknowledgment is made to Dodd, Mead & Company, Inc.,
and McGraw-Hill Ryerson Ltd. for permission to reprint selections
from *The Collected Poems of Robert Service*.

Published by the University of Minnesota Press
111 Third Avenue South, Suite 290
Minneapolis, MN 55401-2520
http://www.upress.umn.edu

Printed in the United States of America on acid-free paper

Library of Congress Cataloging-in-Publication Data
Olson, Sigurd F., 1899–1982
Reflections from the North Country / Sigurd F. Olson ; illustrated
by Leslie Kouba. — 1st University of Minnesota Press ed.
p.   cm. — (The Fesler-Lampert Minnesota heritage book series)
Originally published: 1st ed. New York : Knopf, 1976.
ISBN 0-8166-2993-5 (pbk. : alk. paper)
1. Nature.   I. Title.   II. Series.
QH81.066   1998
508—dc21   98-21094

The University of Minnesota is an equal-opportunity
educator and employer.

10 09 08 07 06 05 04 03 02 01 00 99 98   10 9 8 7 6 5 4 3 2 1

To Ann Langen

CONTENTS

Contents

PART THREE
The Imponderables

ACKNOWLEDGMENTS

I am grateful to my entire family for understanding, patience, and encouragement, especially to Esther for the title *Reflections*; to Ann Langen for her skilled editing, sound judgment, and enthusiastic participation during its preparation and final editing; to Angus Cameron and his staff for invaluable criticism, planning, and organization; and to Alfred A. Knopf, who years ago endorsed the basic idea of the book.

Appreciation for the use of excerpts from many books, articles, and essays goes to: Viking Press, publisher of *The Challenge of Man's Future*, by Harrison Brown; Mentor books for a statement in *Religion Without Revelation*, by Julian Huxley; Random House for several expressions from *Human Nature and the Human Condition*, by Joseph Wood Krutch; Harper & Row for a comment from the *Phenomenon of Man*, by Pierre Teilhard de Chardin; Harcourt Brace Jovanovich for the insight and vision in *The Conduct of Life*, by Lewis Mumford; NBC Television for an interview by Carl Stern with Abraham Joshua Heschel; *Beaver* magazine for permission to use several quotes from an article on Blair Fraser by the author; Columbia University Press for two quotations from *Primitive Views of the World*, edited by Stanley Diamond; Crown publishers for quotations from *Ideas and Opinions*, by Albert Einstein; Scribner's for comments from *The God Within*, by René Dubos; Capricorn Books for two short poems by Lao Tzu as translated by Witter Bynner, also for the statement of Lin Yutang as quoted from the *Wisdom of India and China;* Longmans Green for the use of a brief statement from Le-

Acknowledgments

Compt du Nouy's *Human Destiny;* Macmillan Company for several excerpts from *The Philosophy of Civilization,* by Albert Schweitzer.

I am deeply indebted to the following for the inspiration and the wisdom they have afforded me: Henry David Thoreau, John Galsworthy, William Cullen Bryant, Bertrand Russell, I. W. Heysinger, Aldo Leopold, Loren Eisley, Henry Beston, Father Le Jeune's Diaries, André Malraux, John Burroughs, Ralph Waldo Emerson, William Hazlitt, C. K. Leith, A. R. Cahn, J. E. Potzger, Herman De Costa, A. Y. Jackson, Richard Proenneke, Sir James Jeans, Paul Sears, Robert Sterling North, Walt Whitman, Samuel Taylor Coleridge.

S.F.O.

REFLECTIONS

When a man has traveled the wilderness most of his life, his earliest memories steeped in beauty and the joys such experience gives, when he has watched the changes that have come not only to the land itself but to the people, their attitudes, and the world, now entirely different from the one he first knew, it is only natural to reflect on countless explorations and interpret them in the light of the slow filtrations into consciousness of an almost forgotten way of life. It becomes, in a sense, a distillation of how he feels and looks at things, the development of a point of view that encompasses his understanding of man's long relationship to nature, all living things, and the universe itself.

In a book as brief as this it is impossible to cover everything, but as I go through the process of remembering and trying to invest my recollections with meaning, readers may find the answers to questions they also may have raised. Whether I talk of timelessness, cosmic rhythms, and the slow cycles of seasonal change; or look at such personal things as aliveness, wonder, and wholeness; or attempt to enter the dark infinities of mystery and the unknown—it makes little difference. What really matters is a broad perspective woven through the fabric of them all, the long view of a naturalist and wanderer through wild country and all he has written and thought about over the years.

This collection of essays is a partial summing-up of my personal beliefs, and I hope those who travel with me may hear that almost imperceptible note of harmony that runs through the grand symphony of the land I have known.

S.F.O.

PART ONE

Primal Heritage

*Life in the wilderness can be a
continual contemplation and communion
with God and Spirit of those values
echoing within us all, values born of
timelessness, mystery, the great
silences, and an ancient way of life.*

FRONTIERS

We dream of times when
there was room to breathe,
work to challenge our strength
and courage, a chance for a man
to carve out his destiny.

While I have known many frontiers over the continent, it is the era of the fur trade and exploration in the Northwest that has intrigued me most. I never lost my love of it or the thrill of following those ancient routes and facing the challenges voyageurs met when the Northwest was still unknown. I live at the edge of the famous lake region known as the Quetico-Superior, and as I look across the reaches of a waterway beyond my cabin, I think of the gaily painted birchbark canoes that once crossed those whitecapped expanses on the trail from Lake Vermilion to Grand Portage on Lake Superior.

Coming out of the mouth of the Tamarack two miles to the west, the canoemen paddled toward the entrance to the Burntside River and must have watched for a Lob pine somewhere near my point that would show the way. Sometimes I can almost hear them singing "En Roulant," "La Claire Fontaine," and see red-tipped paddles flashing in the sunlight. That was long ago, but the great areas of the Canadian shield mean more to me because of the adventurous spirit of those early canoemen and the love they had for a wilderness way of life.

I have known the West as well, and followed the old trails, the Oregon, Santa Fe, and Coronado, and even those of the East leading through the passes of the Appalachians, the fading paths of the pioneers who surged away from the first beachheads on the Atlantic coast. So close are we to those frontiers, one can almost hear the rumble and screech of wagon trains and the cries of "Westward ho!" On the plains the ruts of those trails still show, and following them I think of the unlimited space and opportunity of a land once new and unchanged.

We sing the songs of those days, re-create in movies and on television what now seems a Golden Age, dream of times when there was room to breathe, work to challenge our strength and courage, a chance for a man to carve out his destiny. We treasure those memories, but now something is missing and we have lost the sense of direction and purpose we once had. We flounder and wonder where to turn, see stagnation, crowding, and ugliness, with the free spirit of an almost forgotten era gone.

It is good for us to recall the hardihood and simplicities that period represents, for we are still part of those frontiers and will survive because of what they gave us. We must solve the enormous problems that confront us, far bigger ones than we have ever known, but we face them with those sterling qualities woven into our pioneer character. Within us is an inner reserve of power and resilience because of what the frontiers did.

With the romantic era of expansion long past, we ponder the mounting environmental and sociological crisis. Countless panaceas have been expounded, billions spent on possible solutions, but none held the answer to our real dilemma. During the past decade, however, a new pattern of action has been emerging that might hold within itself the key to our predicament. It sprang from the same courage and indomitable resolve that drove wagon trains across hot deserts, forced them through precipitous mountains; from the spirit that carried canoes over endless portages and down dangerous rapids to goals no voyageurs were ever sure could be reached.

We no longer face a physical frontier, but a change in philosophy, a complete reversal of our attitude toward the earth that might open the door to a golden era far more resplendent than the old. Never in man's long evolution have such ideas arisen, never has he had a more dramatic choice or one that could change his life more drastically. It is enlightening to look back beyond the old familiar frontiers into the misty past of the Stone Age, for this is not the first time man has had to make such decisions.

During the past fifty thousand years, he has made three, each of which has influenced his future irrevocably. The first was when he abandoned his former existence of perhaps a million years or so and began to plant seeds and domesticate animals. As he discovered the security of growing his own food and taming creatures he used to hunt, life changed. For thousands of years he continued his nomadic ways to supplement his new activities, but eventually depended more and more on herds and growing crops. We have not forgotten these ways, however, for genetic structures, mutations, and adaptations move very slowly, and within us all there is still evidence of a primitive life which left its indelible mark—far deeper, perhaps, than those of the recent frontiers so fresh in our memories.

The second great decision was inevitably an outgrowth

of the first: a gathering together in family groups, hamlets, villages, and finally cities, with the actual departure from the land by countless millions. The resultant impact on human culture, development, and outlook that came with separation from close involvement with the earth was a new security and leisure, the beginnings of education and class consciousness—a far cry from anything man had ever known. In forgotten cities flourishing from five to six thousand years ago—such as Ur and Babylon, in the valleys of the Tigris and the Euphrates of Mesopotamia; and Thebes and Memphis, in the valley of the Nile—men behind the protection of city walls and armies forgot their old ways and proceeded to build a society of specialization and surplus, a society that produced mathematics, sculpture, art, and writing, with the luxury of time to plan and philosophize.

Most of man's known history is involved with this era, but not until two hundred years ago did he embark on a third major decision, after the invention of the steam engine by James Watt. This relatively simple event spawned the industrial revolution, bringing in its wake all the developments our inventive genius could contrive. Once man chose such a course, the entire civilized world was changed, as was his old way of life in a relatively stable environment. In the process, he cut his spiritual roots to the land and to the interdependencies that over the centuries had preserved the ecosystem of which he was once an integral part.

Now we are on the verge of making the greatest decision of all, a change in the goals and philosophies that brought about the present ecological crises, a complete realignment of our relationship to the earth, a man-land ethic that it is hoped will recognize our responsibilities and stewardship. Until now progress has been measured by things, better organization, and new inventions that increased our affluence, but now we are beginning to think of quality and richness of life rather than quantity. We are asking great questions about our system of values, wondering if the good life can be measured by old standards, if more and more is always better, or if there can be satisfaction with what we have.

We are at last beginning to understand what is at stake. It is more than wilderness, beauty, or peace of mind; it is the survival of man and his culture. Other ages have passed into oblivion; one has only to consider what happened to the fertile lands of Mesopotamia and the hundred dead cities built one on top of the other, the eleven civilizations that simply disappeared, to realize it was not war or pestilence that brought their end, but changing climates, unwise use of the land, and lack of vision. It was then the barbarians moved down from the mountains to destroy the cities, for the people were weakened and had no strength or will to repel disaster.

Where does this leave us, this knowledge of the distant past of our race and our frontiers? We know our basic human needs, that man is part of all that has gone before, his hunger and discontent an inescapable longing for the old simplicities he once knew, that we are in truth children of the earth and cannot change. It is wholeness we are seeking, and being in tune with ancient rhythms and the intangible values of a life we have abandoned.

We also know we cannot forsake our technology, but must find a balance between it and environment. If we can use this tremendous backlog of knowledge to work toward the preservation of the land instead of its desecration, if we can improve the quality of life, change our priorities, achieve balance and understanding of our role as human beings in a complex world, this coming era may well set the stage for a richer civilization than man has ever known. This is the challenge of the new American frontier.

THE GATHERERS

*For uncounted centuries man
was a gatherer and hunter in the
endless search for food. Those
centuries left their mark upon us
all, and when one goes out on a foray
of any kind, ancient reactions surge
out of the depths of our minds.*

For uncounted centuries nomadic man was a gatherer and
a hunter, a gatherer of fruits, roots, and buds, insects, snails,
and lizards—anything edible—in the endless search for food.
To supplement what he foraged, he developed weapons of
the chase and became a hunter as well. Long before he moved
into tribal villages or communes, this was his way of life, as
it is of the few remaining peoples left on earth unaffected by
modern man. For us, too, it is as normal to go on such expeditions as it is to fish or hunt. Those centuries left their
mark upon us all, and when one goes on a foray of any kind,
ancient reactions surge out of our subconscious. Even the
thought of such activity brings a feeling of excitement.

It is as natural as breathing to follow the ebb and flow
of the tides looking for mussels, clams, and crabs, for humans
living close to the sea made full use of its bounty. Men who

need not depend on such largess continue their harvesting with new objectives, which are still meaningful.

Last fall, Elizabeth and I picked blueberries high on the rocky shelves of an island. There on flats made spongy by the moisture washing down from bare cliffs behind them, the ground was blue with berries. At first we picked swiftly, moving from place to place, but gradually became aware of the beauty far below, a cluster of smooth, glaciated little islands, a blaze of maples on the opposite shore, a swamp turning gold in a small bay. While harvesters at heart, we found beauty as well, and with such a display around us it was difficult to concentrate on the berries.

Later in the season, just before the frosts, we picked cranberries in a glacial bog covered with heather now turned to copper. The cranberries lay like jewels in the soft green of sphagnum and it seemed a shame to pick them and disturb their pattern. Wild cranberries are different from the tame, and contain some of the essence of the bog itself, the smell of wet moss and muskeg, a certain tartness lost during the processes of cultivation and care in the artificially controlled water levels of commercial bogs. Perhaps it is just imagination that makes us think there is this difference, but I believe smells and environment in one's gathering do make things taste different. Let us not forget our forebears absorbed all the sights, sounds, and smells that went with their search for food.

The same is true of wild cherries and plums, no matter what their type: plums from the sands of ocean beaches; wild grapes from the South; pin cherries, chokecherries, Indian plum from woodsides, fencerows, or open meadows—all taste different from those raised commercially. Again there is the joy of gathering, the beauty of fruit wherever it is found, and the happiness of preparing it for winter use.

And so it is whenever we go into the woods: there is always the searching, and one never knows what he may find. A long ridge on the forest floor might be all that is left of a giant pine fallen in a storm a century ago; lift off the moss, and if you are lucky find dozens of pine knots so impregnated with resin they have not decayed in the slightest. We treasure them and place them carefully in the packsack. At the cabin they have a special spot in a dry corner of the woodshed where it might be a year before they are ready to burn. When one is laid onto the coals of a dying fire for a final flare of fossil sunlight, we remember many unforgettable things about the day we discovered them under their blanket of moss.

Whenever I go into the woods, I am still the eternal gatherer, always searching the ground. Perhaps it is a whorl of dry birch bark blown off a tree, lying there waiting to be picked up, the splinters of a lightning-struck pine or cedar so dry they would burst into flame at the touch of a match. On our expeditions into the North, we always tuck such treasures into the end of the canoe to use in case of foul weather.

Paddling close to shore constantly watching for the unusual is one of the great dividends of being in a canoe. Once this summer, just at dusk, my grandson Derek and I noticed a dark splotch in the top of an Indian-plum bush of some size. "Porcupine," I said instinctively. We stopped paddling and watched as the animal gathered the still unripened berries and munched them contentedly—another gatherer on the prowl. The longer we sat there, the surer I was the animal was not a porky. Then Derek, whose eyes are better than mine, said, "Do porkies have quills in their tails?" I assured him they did. "But this one hasn't quills. The tail looks furry and is curved around a branch."

I pushed the canoe a little closer, alongside a windfall extending into the water from the plum tree, and to my amazement saw it was a full-grown fisher: the unmistakable doglike face, the rounded little ears, the smooth furry body lying on its thick bed of fruit-laden branches.

"A fisher," I whispered. "Get out on the log and walk toward shore. Use your paddle to steady yourself." He was soon within a few feet of the animal, who was not at all disturbed. The dark was settling and we could barely see it.

"Let's go," I said, "We don't want to scare him." As we left, I told him, "You've seen a fisher, and may never see another as long as you live."

I looked back once, and the animal was eating berries as though we had not been there. Out in the open, the sunset was glowing in the west. "Let's call it Fisher Point," said Derek, and so it will always be to me, the result of a different kind of gathering.

I am also a collector of rocks and my home is full of them, found across the continent from the Quetico-Superior country far into the Arctic and Alaska. Each has special meaning. One before me now is a bit of flat ledge, polished in some stream into a smooth oval and grown with the orange lichen common on the tundras of the caribou country north of the tree line. It brings back endless vistas of open space, the sight of caribou swimming in lakes and rivers. The orange lichen has not changed color and I have only to moisten it with my tongue to bring its brilliance back.

Another is a small piece of uranium ore the color of cobalt, the formation that foretold the discovery of a vast deposit on Great Bear Lake, just south of the Arctic coast. Cobalt bloom, the geologists called it, the hue that gave away the secret of Eldorado.

The other day in Anchorage, I went into a native art shop full of paintings, carvings, and native crafts. Again I was gathering, and found a tiny ivory figurine, a reminder of all that is truly Alaskan. This, too, is part of the ancient seeking of the past, only in this case it was purely the search for beauty and meaning in the work of those who are closer to the old wilderness than we—and, without question, more perceptive of its meanings.

In the summer there is a constant search for flowers in Alaska: the yellow tundra poppies, the fireweeds, the mallows, the heather—the succession of blooms I know so well at home. In the spring, the first haze of Nile green of aspen on the hillsides; in the fall, the first color of leaves, a blaze of maple alone on a shore still green, a tussock of grasses golden in the sun.

We are all harvesters and hunters, always looking and hoping for something that will give pleasure to the senses or might be worth keeping for some reason, and just possibly be good to eat. Many—and perhaps countless—generations will pass before this urge disappears. It is my wish we will never lose it, that every trip away from home will be one of adventure and excitement, for no matter what we gather, deep within us is the same primitive satisfaction our ancestors knew.

One has only to watch the shell collectors along the beaches of Hawaii, Florida, or the Caribbean to know how deeply ingrained this instinct is. Thousands comb the beaches in the eternal quest of beautiful shells, bits of coral, anything the mighty waves and tides have brought ashore. It becomes an obsession with some, and they are out early in the morning to find the best before other collectors get there. It is the unexpected that makes it so fascinating. I have a beautiful cowrie, with its color as fresh as when I found it in Hawaii, smooth, polished, and unbroken, a gem worth keeping. This gathering goes deep in the lives of natives of the South Seas, and the necklaces and decorations they make of them are beautiful. At one time the cowrie was used for barter, and when I look at mine I know it is priceless; it is rich with the memory of soft breezes, azure waters, and the endless sound of the surf.

NOMADS

It was all joy and romance
traveling with my French-Canadian friend Pierre.
We were actors on an ancient stage where
the voyageur was a symbol and way of life—
the gay spirit with which he faced enormous
odds and a love of the wilderness few
frontiersmen ever knew.

I watched a couple of canoes beating their way across the open reaches of the lake. The boys in them were singing and I caught snatches of their song. Stripped to the waist, they were using their brawn to keep the slender craft from getting out of line in the gale. Traveling by primitive means, I knew within them the long inheritance of a nomadic ancestry was surging through their minds and bodies, bringing back the joy of movement and travel, adrenalin pouring into their veins, giving courage to muscles being strained to the utmost. If I had been close enough, I might have heard the laughter in their song, seen the glad light in their eyes. They were at home, doing what men had done for uncounted centuries!

I noticed this phenomenon early in life, during my guiding days. As soon as men forgot complexities and problems, the ancient joy took hold. Men who had never sung a note before bellowed songs into the teeth of the wind; faces that at the start showed grimness and strain soon began to relax.

I remember one trip in particular with a doctor named Sydney Knowles, who had a good tenor voice. When we paddled together, he would lead off and soon we would come into full harmony, and at night after things were put away we sang all the old songs we knew. During a season with the Wisconsin Geological Survey, we had the good fortune to have another tenor with us. Each evening we harmonized, for we were in the bush and it was the natural thing to do. Whenever there were settlers around, men and women would come to hear us and, to our delight, often joined in. My memories are not of those long days running survey lines, the miles and miles of rough country we covered, the topographical maps we prepared, the streams and watersheds we traced, but the music of our quartet. I recall some of them now: "Honey, Honey, Bless Your Heart," "Shenandoah," "The Missouri Waltz," "Sleep, Kentucky Babe"—they will echo forever.

I have noticed when traveling with Indians that they often break into song when on the move. Morose and unhappy in camp and often irritable with the drudgery and work of preparation, once they were on the trail things changed and they sang and, after supper was over, made music as only Indians can. Eskimos are the same, and though we cannot always understand their music, the joy and rhythm are there.

Often on expeditions some phrase or word, some inference comes into play that puts a different light on everything. While I was traveling with a French Canadian, Pierre LaRonge, we often spoke in the patois of Quebec, his homeland. During our trips, I became François and we saw the world of our wilderness as two Canucks. Before long other members of the group would fall in with us, and our travels became one with the voyageurs of old. I can still hear Pierre say, "Dose pack, she's too heavee for poor Pierre," or, speaking of prunes, "De prune ees de finest berry what grows een de swamp." Or, "When you catch dose trout, use hoppergrass or hanger worm," and when the beaver had flooded a portage with their dams, "Dose bevaire, she's a fine animal."

It was at night when we joined in old French chansons and really felt like voyageurs, for we sang the same music that had drifted across the open lakes in the days of the old brigades.

But Pierre was at his best reciting some of the poetry of those early days.

> "De win' she blow on Lac St. Claire
> She blow den blow some more.
> Eef you don' drown on dees beeg lac,
> You better kip close to shore."

The one he loved best was "The Voyageur," by Henry Drummond. All would go well until the last verses, then his eyes grew round and dark, his voice husky as he declaimed:

> "So dat's de reason I drink tonight
>   To de men of de Grand Nor'west
>   For hees heart was young, an hees heart was light
>   So long as he's leevin dere—
>
> I'm proud of the sam blood in my vein,
>   I'm a son of de Nort' Win' wance again—
>   So we'll fill her up til de bottle's drain
>   An' drink to de Voyageur."

It was all joy and romance traveling with Pierre LaRonge. We were actors on an ancient stage where the voyageur was a symbol and way of life—the gay spirit with which he faced enormous odds and a love of the wilderness few frontiersmen ever knew.

Sometimes during the winter months between trips, I would visit men I had guided during the summer, and what gay occasions they were. Gone was any memory of the hard and often desperate days. The highlights were the good ones we remembered most vividly. We sang the old songs over and over again, told the threadbare jokes and laughed as though we were hearing them for the first time. This was the afterglow of the happy times we had known together in the bush.

When I think back over the many trips I've made in far parts of the land, it is always the same. One is a trip in the Blue Range country of New Mexico, where I traveled with an old lion hunter over the red-rock canyons and plateaus when there were still mountain lions, pumas, or catamounts for the taking. The moon happened to be full during the expedition, and I shall never forget sitting around a fragrant fire of mesquite or cedar listening to the hunter's tales. Again the music, this time with a guitar accompaniment, as we sang the old ditties of the wagon trains and mountain men.

I remember Bruce Neal, then in his eighties, one of the last of the mountain men, and his amazement at the way I rode a horse. "Sig," he said one day, "you've done a lot of ridin', ain't you?" "No, Neal," I said, "I haven't ridden much of anything but canoes, but I've traveled a good many thousand miles that way." "Well," he answered, "I knew you had ridden something, the way you seem to be a part of your horse. When he leans, you lean the other way, when he goes down a gully you're part of him, all a matter of balance and being part of the cayuse you're ridin'." From that moment on we laughed about my riding, and I sat a little taller in the saddle because of it.

On a caribou survey in northern Manitoba, with Eskimos to help with the tagging on Lake Nejanilini, it was no different. At night when we sat around a fire of scrub white spruce, we would pick up a radio station in Montreal and listen to the rock-and-roll music, and the Eskimo boys would jump to their feet and do a dance as wild and beautiful as any I had ever seen. Theirs, too, was a joy of being in the bush chasing caribou, and while dancing they sang songs I did not know, and left me with the same feeling of peace I'd always found along the outtrails of the world.

I made a canoe trip once on the Current River in the Ozarks, starting at Jack's Fork above the Current and down that winding rapid-filled stream to the White River below. There were four of us from different parts of the country making a survey of the river with the possibility of its ultimate establishment as the first wild river in America. That river was a continuous series of rather swift but mild rapids, a joyous adventure, and when something happened there was plenty to laugh about, as when we approached a sweeper reaching so far out I could not avoid it. Just high enough above the water to catch either the bow of the canoe or the bowman himself, it lay in wait for us, and as we neared I saw it was my bowman who would get it. Try as I might, I could not pull out far enough to save him, and as we ran swiftly toward the swaying treetop, it plucked him neatly out of the canoe and left him hanging across it. Fortunately my end of the canoe drifted out and I escaped. The water was cold, for it was spring, but when we got together again the humor of the situation made us laugh: the picture of him hanging like a wet rag on a swaying sweeper. Before the trip was over, there were many incidents, all different, but they made our days and nights live with the sheer fun of our encounters.

It is one of the secrets of happy travel to see the humor

that comes to the surface when it is needed, and is often the saving grace in what could otherwise have been a miserable experience. There is nothing worse than to travel with someone who cannot see the ludicrous in any happening. Nomads as we are, it is humor that may sometimes make the difference between life and death.

I think of "Oh, Susanna" on the treks West, "Green Sleeves" and the songs of Stephen Foster about the Suwannee River, which I followed with my old friend Frank Masland from its source in the Okefenokee Swamp almost to tidewater on the west Florida coast.

It was February and the first blossoms were coming out, the redbuds and the forsythia and honeysuckle, but because it was early the nights were cold. One of those nights, separated from our sleeping bags and tents, we slept in the open behind a windbreak of palmetto, with the bitter wind lashing us and a fire barely able to hold its own against the gale. We were sitting there shivering, curled up as best we could with a single poncho to cover us, when Frank said, "I've been happier, but I can't remember where." That became our theme song all the way. No matter what the adventure, and there were many, one of us would say, "I've been happier, but I can't remember where."

Every canoe trip produced some gem, "You can't fool a horsefly," "No matter how wet and cold you are, you're always warm and dry," "Those beans are hard, but I like 'em that way."

I have come to feel laughter and fun on the trails may be the secret of the joy of travel, as when one of my companions, Blaire Fraser, bellowed into an Arctic wind north of Great Slave a seaman's ditty he loved: "Once I had a Spanish gal, and boy she was a dandy," that song somehow took the bite out of the wind.

INTUITION

*It is when one reaches
down into the dark realms of the
past that creative ideas surge
forth.*

Intuition is different from instinct, the latter being a response to physical and physiological stimuli. When one is confronted with sudden danger, adrenalin pours into the body in preparation for battle, flight, evasive action. When the hair rises on one's neck and one is conscious of being followed or facing the unknown, reactions to such fears are instinctive.

Intuition is the response of the subconscious mind arising from the depths of that vast pool of racial awareness which encompasses all experience, not only of our own species but of the forms from which we have come. Students of the brain are convinced we operate only in the upper tenth of our gray matter; below it, like an iceberg, is a vast storage network of memories embodying all man has ever thought or experienced.

An officer in the British Air Force once told me that aces are born, not made. "We can train fine flyers," he said, "but when the crunch comes, only those who act automatically survive to become aces. Somehow," he continued, "an automatic pilot takes over and a man with such a response to a crisis does not have to think. Something does the thinking for him."

People who are intuitive have the edge over those who are not. We hear much these days about extrasensory perception and the natural responses of individuals to others—an almost uncanny sense of knowing that comes when inhibitions are eliminated and people act with deeper perception than is ordinarily the case. In the same category are those who have the ability to prophesy and predict events, the sense of knowing something has happened or is going to happen. Such feelings are more common among those who have lived away from civilization: Indians, trappers, and guides. I recall the story of two trappers spending the winter in a remote outpost cabin. Running short of food they decided the time had come to take one of the two dog teams and travel some two hundred miles for supplies. The partner who stayed with the second team told of the reactions of the home dogs; as the day approached for the return, how they began to sense something, spent hours down at the landing watching and waiting, all but exploding with excitement while the other team was still many miles away.

I have seen horses hesitate before crossing a bridge they considered unsafe, have watched Indians skirt ice that looked perfectly solid to anyone else and have been with them when they sensed the coming of wind or storm, or an aura of impending doom. This is something modern man seems to have lost because senses have been dulled by the constant erosion and distraction of today's life.

I talked to a young teacher at Moose Factory, below James Bay, who was amazed at what the Cree Indian children could sense and feel when he went with them into the bush. Approaching a group of partridge, they sensed where the birds were long before they were flushed—not an instinctive reaction, but one of keenness and observation combined, perhaps, with intuition.

Indians, woodsmen, farmers, and all those who spend their lives out-of-doors can smell the weather. This sense is not prompted by arthritic twinges or meteorological knowledge, but a certain something way down deep.

Not long ago, I visited with a young Cherokee Indian who came from an important tribe in the Southeast, one that developed a culture far in advance of others, with perceptions woven into their legendry and religious beliefs. We were talking about this, and to illustrate a point he picked up a stone and held it in his hands.

"If you hold this stone long enough," he said, "it will speak to you and tell you that there are no enemies where you are going; that all you meet are your friends. The stone talks to you not with words, as white men or other Indians, but in a language which needs no words."

What he actually was saying is that real communication is not dependent on words or language, but is an interplay between the mind of man and inanimate objects, something great students of the human mind are just now beginning to understand.

An old prospector friend of mine, Harry Moody, wrote me just before he died near Flin Flon, Manitoba, that we could sit across a fire from each other and carry on a conversation without saying a word. "I know what you think," he said, "and you know what I think. It is enough just to be together sitting around a fire. We do not have to tell each other our thoughts or what we might be going to do."

Extrasensory perception, thought transference, micromagnetic waves—it makes little difference what we call it, but we know it occurs and we often have proof. We have just begun to touch the fringes of this type of knowledge, and it has opened a broad new field of investigation.

It may never be possible to explain completely what happens, how the human brain can know or transmit thoughts or messages. Many scientific minds are exploring the possibilities and, as usual, most people scoff at and ridicule the veracity of evidence. In a sense this exploration is in line with the current effort to communicate with life in outer space. Nothing may ever come of it but one can never tell. Stranger things have been found in the research programs of many fields.

I have often mentioned the experience of feeling that somewhere or sometime I have done a particular thing before. This often comes when I've been on the trail, when the life I have been leading seems more natural than the one I left back in the town. This is perception, this reaching down into the depths of consciousness.

What does perception mean to modern man, how can he nurture these desiccated nerve ends of his ancient knowing and make them flower again into a fuller life, with more appreciation of beauty and awareness and the potentialities of our relationships to others? There are ways this can be done: by placing oneself in the proper situation and mood, and willfully recognizing there is something we possess that is normally hidden and lost to the modern mind.

I recall, when writing at white heat, the utter amazement I felt on reading something I had written, and saying, "Now where did that come from?" Thoreau felt somewhat the same when he said, "It is like going fishing. One never knows what one will catch." Writing at its best must come from deep within, for often there is where truth and originality lie; none comes entirely from the upper tenth of gray matter. It is when one reaches down into the dark realms of the past that great ideas surge forth.

Cultivation of perception and intuition makes life more meaningful and worth nurturing. I know nothing about the transmigration of souls, but if it is interpreted as dipping down into what may be former lives, then there may be substance to the belief. It is enough for me to know how vital intuition is to our happiness, how important to be alive and aware not only of our environment but of people and other creatures. So often we go through life operating on our instincts, barring ourselves from the richness that is or could be ours if we willed.

Wisdom is the key to a fuller life. If a richer one for me is enjoying my environment to the fullest, then it is up to me to cultivate my awareness of all I see.

In our world with the fabric of technology and our way of life seemingly falling apart, this may be a key to sanity and equilibrium. We may have to change and live more frugally without some of our comforts. Perhaps it would be better if we did not eat so well, had more physical work, walked more and rode less, contented ourselves with ideas and other goals rather than with material things. While I know the crises confronting us now, somehow while I am at my cabin, it does not seem of such catastrophic importance as it does in the confused uncertainty we feel today. Out there I am convinced we must trust those intuitive perceptions that have guided mankind in the past; listen to our hunches, in backwoods parlance, for they may be the way of wisdom after all.

TIMELESSNESS

*When one finally arrives at
the point where schedules are
forgotten, and becomes immersed
in ancient rhythms, one begins
to live.*

Our lives seem governed by speed, tension, and hurry.
We move so fast and are caught so completely in a web of
confusion there is seldom time to think. Our cities are veri-
table beehives dominated by the sounds of traffic and industry.
Even at the top of the highest building, one is conscious of the
hive's human busyness.

The change of seasons is often unobserved, the coming of
winter, spring, summer, and autumn. Winter merely means
an aggravation of traffic and transportation, spring the sloshi-
ness of rain, summer dust and heat, fall the withering of
transplanted flowers and the threat of cold. For one who has
lived in the wilderness, it is impossible to adjust to this, and
each time I come away from the city, I feel drained of silence
and naturalness.

During a trip into the wilds, it often takes men a week or
more to forget the frenetic lives they have led, but inevitably
the feeling of timelessness does come, often without warning.

On a trip long ago, I remember the first impact of a rising full moon. We were in the open on a great stretch of water, with islands in the far distance. The sky gradually brightened and an orange slice of moon appeared; we watched as the great sight unfolded before us. At that moment, the city men in the party caught a hint of its meaning. They were entranced as the moon became clear: pulsating as though alive, it rose slowly above the serrated spruces of the far shore. Then, as it almost reluctantly paled, we took to our paddles again. We searched and searched and found a long point from which we could see both sunset and moonrise at the same time. The calling of the loons meant more after that, and as the dusk settled all were aware of something new in their lives.

I know now as men accept the time clock of the wilderness, their lives become entirely different. It is one of the great compensations of primitive experience, and when one finally reaches the point where days are governed by daylight and dark, rather than by schedules, where one eats if hungry and sleeps when tired, and becomes completely immersed in the ancient rhythms, then one begins to live.

For uncounted millennia man lived this way; only under the stress of danger and the activity of the chase was it violated, and then just for short periods. Life went along as smoothly and gradually as the rising of the moon. It is this long inheritance that governs us in spite of our supposed sophistication. No wonder we have nervous breakdowns and depend on artificial calming devices to sleep and quiet down.

It is not surprising city dwellers leave their homes each weekend and head for beaches, mountains, or plains where they can recapture the feeling of timelessness. It is this need, as much as scenery or just getting out of town, that is the reason for their escape. In the process, however, they may still be so imbued with the sense of hurry and the thrill of travel that they actually lose what they came to find. Many tour the national parks with the major objective of getting as many park stickers as possible in the short time available, and what should have been a leisurely experience becomes a race to include all the areas within reach. When such travelers return, they are often wearier than when they started.

I shall never forget a young couple who roared into a lookout spot of the Grand Canyon just at dusk when it was at its most spectacular, with the last slanting rays of the sun touching the tops of pinnacles with gold just before they darkened into the deep blues and lavenders of night. Several of us had been waiting for an hour, feasting on a panorama unequaled anywhere in the world, and over it was a silence and timelessness that gave added meaning to the scene.

Without warning, a car door slammed and the couple hurried to where we were. In a moment the girl said, "Well, we've seen this one. Let's try to make it to the next before we call it a day," and off they sped into the night. I know they were disappointed, for tension and activity were really their goal. They were doing what so many do: "killing time," as though time were inexhaustible and could be wasted at will.

In the wilderness there is never this sense of having to move, never the feeling of boredom if nothing dramatic happens. Time moves slowly, as it should, for it is a part of beauty that cannot be hurried if it is to be understood. Without this easy flowing, life can become empty and hectic.

Not long ago, as I was sitting beside my cabin, a mink came along the shore followed by three half-grown young. They were in and out of the water, slipping over rocks and between roots, and their movements were grace personified. They did not see me, nor were they conscious of my scent, for I was hidden by a clump of hazel and the wind was from the shoreline. They soon disappeared in their eternal search for food, or perhaps just for the joy of movement.

That afternoon I paddled down a river, flowing through mats of sedges, with towering hills toward the north. A golden eagle soared high above the ridges, gliding without effort on the wind currents over the valley. As I watched the huge bird, I could not help but feel I was part of its lazy movement, of the sky and the wind, looking down over its domain as eagles had done for centuries, when only Indians were there to mark its flight, or voyageurs in birchbark canoes on the way from Lake Vermilion to Shagawa Lake and the border.

With natives one is more conscious of this sense of timelessness. They look at us with puzzlement, wondering why we hurry so desperately. In Hawaii a year ago I saw a native Polynesian standing on a sandy shore where the surf came in. He was alone, bronzed and calm, just listening to the endless roar as the glistening combers struck the reefs outside. He had his surfboard and I knew he had been part of the scene for hours, possibly all day long. If he had been a white, he might have thought of taking one more ride, but he merely stayed there quietly, reluctant to leave.

In the Far North of this continent, I have known Indians and Eskimos and have sensed ancient rhythms with them, the feeling of endless time, and I sometimes think the reason we do not understand them is because they listen to a different drummer and see no purpose in the constant pushing and rush. Back of this sense of unlimited time is an entirely different philosophy of life from ours.

We cannot all live in the wilderness, or even close to it, but we can, no matter where we spend our lives, remember the background which shaped this sense of the eternal rhythm, remember that days, no matter how frenzied their pace, can be calm and unhurried. Knowing we can be calm and un-hurried we can refuse to be caught in the so-called rat race and the tension which kills Godlike leisure. Though conscious of the roar around us, we can find peace if we remember we all came from a common mold and primeval background. It is when we forget and divorce ourselves entirely from what man once knew that our lives may spin off without meaning.

SOLITUDE

*Wilderness can be appreciated
only by contrast, and solitude
understood only when we have been
without it.*

Just before freeze-up, a friend of mine, Bob Malkovsky, took a canoe trip through the Quetico-Superior. A veteran canoeman, he had made a number of trips in the past here and in other regions, but this time decided to go alone, and when I asked him about it, he said: "When you're alone, you have time to do things without thinking of anyone else. If you want to go exploring and climb some high ridge instead of paddling, you may. Many times I've looked at a ridge and wondered how it would seem being way on top of it, feasting my eyes for an hour or two or a whole day, or climbing to some barren slope where perhaps no man had ever been. If you want to enjoy a bit of shoreline, seeing the colored leaves swirl around in a little eddy, how the grasses have turned, or watch a beaver storing food in the pile beside his lodge, you can do it."

He continued, "One day I watched an otter with a couple of kits playing on a sandy beach. I was well hidden but could see them perfectly. How long I sat there I don't know, but time made no difference. The little family cavorted around, investigating everything of interest, occasionally taking to the water, the mother talking to her young ones, then back to the beach rolling around and playing like kittens.

"If the weather were foul, I could hole up in my tent and read the whole day long, or if it were moonlight and I felt like paddling, I could travel listening to the night sounds, watching the way of the moon with trees and rocks, and at times cruising down the whole length of its path.

"What's more, you have time to think," he concluded. "I got more out of this trip than any I had ever taken. It opened up new vistas I'd never dreamed about, sharpened my sensibilities and made me more alive."

I have traveled as my friend did many times, and while I love to have companions with me, I discovered long ago what psychologists call "creative silence": the impact of solitude on the mind, the awakening of ideas and thoughts normally hidden when one is with others, the emergence of concepts often lost owing to interruptions and responsibilities. During such times, one drinks from the deep wells of the past.

Something I have often done is to take a bit of poetry or philosophy out of my medicine bag, as I call it, fragments gathered over the years, lay it on a pack before me anchored firmly with a stone, and read it line by line, with time enough to savor every word. This is the way reading should be done, but there is seldom unbroken time or lack of interference that shatters one's absorption.

What did Santayana mean when he said, "I paced the pillared cloisters of the mind," and Arthur O'Shaughnessy when he declared, "We are the music-makers / And we are the makers of dreams"? What did Sir James Jeans, the great astronomer, mean when he said, "The more I contemplate the Universe, the more it seems like a great thought"? What did they really mean—"the pillared cloisters of the mind"? Who are the makers of dreams, what the great thought? Paddling along watching the skies, clouds, and horizons, there is time to mull such thoughts deeply and translate them not in one's own mind, but in the timeless background of hills and distance, the eternal and the immutable.

Everyone needs such quiet times, some solitude to recoup his sense of perspective. One does not have to be in a canoe or in some remote wilderness. I find such times at night when I do much of my reading, but to me when solitude is part of wilderness it comes more surely and with greater meaning. Since the time when man often traveled alone, hunting and foraging, all this became part of him. It is easy to slip back into the ancient grooves of experience.

When I am fly-fishing for brook trout, alone on some favorite stream, the sense of hurry is gone and time seems endless. With no worry about meeting a companion or having a rendezvous at a certain spot, I can stand in one place for hours watching the rising trout, the action of insects over the water, the mayflies, a caddis worm with its strange covering of tiny pebbles or sticks crawling along a rock. Birds come and go, squirrels scurry up and down the pines and spruces. Trout fishing for me is not the taking of fish, but being at one with the stream and all the sights and sounds. The great Leonardo da Vinci said in 1512, "The eye, which is called the window of the soul, is the chief means whereby the understanding may most fully and abundantly appreciate the infinite works of nature, and the ear is the second, inasmuch as it acquires its importance from the fact it hears the things which the eye has seen." I have often thought of that, and wondered if this most perceptive of minds had ever stood in a quiet pool as I have.

While I have not fired a rifle for decades, I still like to

roam the snow-clad hills of November, but now my goal is only to enjoy it and remember.

Not long ago I read an article entitled "The Perimeter Men," those who refuse to live in towns and cities and are always found far from their own kind. The writer, an Alaskan with nearly twenty-five years of experience in roaming the wilds, said as far as he knew there were no more than three hundred perimeter men in all Alaska, men who had truly gone into the bush to find solitude, freedom, and independence. He may have missed some of them far back in the wilds, but he may also be fairly close to the truth. There are short-time perimeter men who go in for a few days or weeks, like my friend Bob, but not many go in forever. There have always been perimeter men along the fringes of civilization all over the world, men who could not live within it long, if at all.

I have known many of them in my lifetime, and know that solitude and all it implies is the main reason for them to forsake their kind. Most seem happy and content, but I wonder if their lives are as full and complete as they think they are, if it is possible to live entirely away from one's own and enjoy life to the fullest. Perhaps they are like the wise men of old who went to the wilderness to meditate and to meet their God. I do not know, but I believe as long as we have only one life to live, it is a pity not to share it with others. Wilderness can be appreciated only by contrast, and solitude understood only when we have been without it. We cannot separate ourselves from society, comradeship, sharing, and love. Unless we can contribute something from wilderness experience, derive some solace or peace to share with others, then the real purpose is defeated.

My son Sig, who has lived in Alaska for a long time, tells of a recluse who had seen no one for several years. The only book he had was the Bible and he was hungry to talk about it.

He knew it from beginning to end, could quote long passages, but the shocking thing was it left him with only one conclusion, that "the Bible is a pack of lies." Instead of seeing the beauty of the Great Book, savoring its rich philosophy, he had become embittered and ingrown. Solitude meant an atrophying of his mind and loss of the human qualities that make men different from beasts. He had traveled the long road back to the primitive and had failed.

One cannot go back for long periods without some personal loss. I discovered this long ago, and have known perimeter men all over the continent who feel the same. Not all of them atrophy; some are keen and delightful, full of joy and without bitterness. But even these men lose something, a certain warmth and humanity, love for others, and the honing of the mind that comes through contact with people. Though they might love other creatures and the land, there is still something missing.

I have had my share of solitude and know whereof I speak. It is beautiful to me, for it brings back perspective and the sense of timelessness. I come back to the friends I have left, stronger, better, and happier than when I went away. If there is writing to do, my thoughts run more smoothly than before; my perceptions and understanding of life's problems more uncluttered after the cleansing powers of solitude.

THE GREAT
SILENCES

*The great silences are beyond
ordinary sounds of nature, a hush
embedded in the deep pool of racial
consciousness.*

The great silences mean more than stillness. They are the
ancient overpowering silences this planet knew before the
advent of modern man. They included the temporary physical
sounds of wind and falling water, the roar and crashing of
prehistoric creatures, natural in origin and always present.
The silence itself was beyond the ordinary sounds of nature;
it dealt with distance, timelessness, and perception, a sense of
being engulfed by something greater where minor sounds
were only a part, a hush embedded in our consciousness.

Today this ancient silence is increasingly difficult to find,
for wherever we go, even in the Far North, there are jet trails
of aircraft miles overhead, and though the plane may not be
seen we can hear the roar, see the contrails hanging motion-
less long afterward, reminding us the silence has been broken.

During the summer, on any lake close to civilization one
is conscious of the roar of motors, but there are occasions
when the old silence returns, when no one is abroad and the
land for a moment is alone. This happens just before freeze-

up, when the tourists have left and it is too cold and dangerous for small boats or other craft to be on the water; again in the spring, when the ice is no longer safe for snowmobiles, snowshoeing, or skiing, when skiplanes cannot land because of open leads. Then for a time the great silence returns.

I sat at the end of a point beyond my cabin one day just before breakup. The leads were wider now, the ice beginning to move, and there was a whispering along the shore where it drifted against the rocks. A pair of seagulls came in, looking for a fish that might have washed up after the long winter. It was good to see their flash of white as they wheeled in the sunlight. I knew they would go to the little rocky islands a mile away where they had always nested, but now they were searching the shores for its bounty, anything that had not survived the whiteness. On Lake Superior, where they had been, there was plenty of food; they could have waited another two weeks, but had responded to the ancient urge to move north to establish their nesting site before it was too late.

Several ravens circled high above, searching for a possible deer carcass hidden by the snows of winter. The squirrels were out and one of them watched from a branch of red pine above, its cones buried in the fall now in plain view, piles of them for the taking. It scolded me, then madly scrambled around the tree. From the south came the squawk of the ravens gathering to feed.

Outside of such pleasant reminders of spring there was nothing, only that all-pervading sense of continuity which ordinary quiet does not give. Quiet is a temporary thing, the old silence ageless. It is the background of man's inherent feeling for the earth, part of his inner self and of the cosmic point of view, the core of mysticism, of religious belief, and of myth and legend.

It is a difficult thing to put into words or on canvas and few artists are successful in catching it. I once saw a painting of a young Indian girl sitting on a ledge overlooking a dark misty canyon in the Southwest. She was alone; the deep gorge was full of silence. I, too, sensed what engulfed her. She was attuned, and no doubt heard the soft background rushing of a rapids far below, or the twittering of a canyon wren. This was more than quiet, something that had no beginning or end, the great primeval hush the land once knew.

Our senses are synchronized to the great quiet by millions of years, making it possible to hear things that today are forgotten. So responsive can we become, even the slightest movement of grasses, leaves, or insects is part of our aware-ness, until it seems we are hearing with our skin, our sight, smell, and touch, for these are part of the overall pervading silences of the past.

Once, in a favorite trout stream, I stood hip deep casting a rise in a darkening pool. A whitethroat called, but the only other sound was the soft rushing of water around my boots. The old silence was there. Then I heard voices and laughter and the sound of paddles against a canoe, and in a moment the silence was gone.

At night I often walk in our yard. The town below is quiet but around is silence, above me the stars and planets. In spring or fall, the calling of migrating birds is high above, and beyond that the blaze of Orion, the Big Dipper, and the cluster of the Pleiades. I can see the twinkle of lights through the trees, but there is no sound of traffic or voices during the lone hours before dawn. My hilltop was once a stand of pine, and a little creek gurgled its way through the gully nearby on its way to the beaver pond below. In those days caribou and moose came there to drink.

I believe mechanical equipment of all kinds should be

kept out of the wilderness, for it is foreign to silence. One can live with people traveling the wilds in primitive ways, but not with aircraft, snowmobiles, or outboards, no matter how muted they may be. Silence is one of the most important parts of a wilderness experience; without it the land is nothing more than rocks, trees, and water.

It includes the rushing of water, the crash of waves against the shore, the roar of avalanches on mountain slopes, of wind through the trees, the howling of wolves, the bugling of elk when the aspen are gold in the foothills, the myriad sounds of birds and insects. At times there seem to be no natural sounds at all, but these are rare. It is only when the silence is broken by the sounds of man's activities that the spell is lost. Natural sounds I welcome: the groan of ice as it accommodates itself to the bed it must keep all winter, or the swish of it as it melts in the spring; the glide of skis over the surface in midwinter, or the soft crunch of snowshoes and the creak of their straps.

When man feels tension as though he were being pulled out of his ancient mold, it is his divorcement from silence that is often responsible, silence built into the fabric of his mind. He may not know what is wrong, but he has only to find it again to restore his equilibrium.

When I return from any wilderness expedition, it is always a shock to encounter the sounds of civilization. It is almost as though I had stepped into a different world, so swift and strident does it seem. When it is more than I can bear, I stroll into the nearby woods to recapture what I had left behind.

MYSTERY AND
THE UNKNOWN

If we can somehow retain
places where we can always
sense the mystery of the unknown,
our lives will be richer.

One day in the Far North, I paddled many miles down a great waterway. The wind was behind me, just a breath, but enough to make paddling easy and almost effortless. I watched vague islands gradually assume form, and points beginning to jut out from the mainland. I was alone with my thoughts, completely engrossed, and almost mesmerized with the idea of the unknown and the whole fascinating concept of mystery.

The notes I had chosen from my wallet to read that day were about the primitive written of by Owen Barfield. He spoke of the nature-linked collective consciousness of magic and mysticism, of totemic thinking and tribally ritualistic participation of most primitives and how all this still reverberates within us. His point of view was my own, a conclusion I had reached long before, that mystery and the unknown were truly the lure of wilderness travel. I also agreed with him that when modern man detaches himself from nature and develops his powers of manipulative control, he loses that felt union with the inner origins of outward forms which constitute perception of their real meanings.

The wind shifted and my almost illegible clipping fluttered dangerously so I secured it more firmly with the extra paddle. Perhaps here, I thought, was what the modern world was all about: man has lost for the moment his union with the past; this is the reason for the unrest and frustration of many people, their loss of contact, the root of their sense of fear and insecurity through having abandoned the ancient state of oneness.

I replaced Barfield with a clipping from Stanley Diamond, the anthropologist.

"The idea of the primitive," he said, "is as old as civilization, because civilization creates it in the search for human identity. This was already evident in the works of Herodotus, Tacitus, Ovid, Horace, and Hesiod, and other poets and scholars of Western classical antiquity: they tried to grasp the nature of their own ancestry and conceptualize the barbarian strangers who thronged the borders of their archaic states. . . . In seeking to understand the primitive world from which they descended and which echoes all around them, they had to sound the depths of their own actual or potential experience."

As I swung my paddle, the miles went by with the horizon growing more and more distinct: this was exactly what I was trying to do.

Diamond said, "The search for the primitive is the search for the utopia of the past, projected into the future; it is paradise lost and paradise regained. . . . It is birth, death, and transcendent rebirth . . . the metaphor of human growth felt in the vast pulse of history."

The shores were close and I had to pick up my precious slips of paper and place them again where they would be safe. Though the first headland was still miles away, I had to find a protected spot for the tent and the canoe. Thinking of supper ahead, I opened my pack, took a trolling line out, and, as I passed between a cluster of islands, dropped a bright copper spoon into the blue-green depths. Going through the narrows, I had a strike and brought to the surface a beautiful sparkling trout, hard and cold, its underside blushed with color, enough for several meals.

Even after landing I could not forget what I had thought about during the afternoon, the search for the primitive, the lure of the unknown—and how good it was to have had the time to really think about it, with my own thoughts reinforced by those of others. During those hours, I had entered the unknown itself, had passed with Barfield and Diamond through the gates of a far horizon, which was still holding me in its grasp.

I am not an anthropologist and have written no scientific tomes on the primitive world, but I have read widely and have known primitive peoples, and believe I have found the secrets of a certain peace and communion with their world. It has disturbed me to see how swiftly they are contaminated by white men and their ways and how they lose their culture and belief. While the elderly may cling to ancient ways, the young are soon weaned, and want nothing of the past.

This is true all over the North, and, having just returned from Alaska, it is particularly vivid to me. I knew of deteriorating native villages coming into contact with the enormous and destructive activities of the pipeline corridors to the North Slope beyond the Brooks Range; I realized such corridors would proliferate with the growing exploration for oil. An early explorer noticed this long ago and spoke of the change that came over an Eskimo village when a missionary gave some steel needles to the wife of the chief, and how much more efficient they were than those of bone used for centuries, with thread instead of sinew. Immediately there was jealousy and envy and a certain class distinction the villagers had never felt before. Once natives become dependent on white man's food and equipment, the old way of life is doomed forever. When they have known government relief, they lose their independence. Young people who spend the winter months going to school outside, preparing themselves for tasks there is no need for back in the villages, are lost. In a few isolated pockets of the Canadian North and in Alaska there is still a clinging to the old ways, but it will not be for long.

Why build skin boats when you can buy better ones of aluminum, plastic, or wood; why paddle when you can use an outboard motor, feed dogs when snowmobiles are much faster and convenient, wear skin clothing or mukluks when you can buy down jackets and felt-lined rubber boots?

The primitive days are passing swiftly and without any seeming regret by the natives themselves, who are suddenly removed from the hardship and insecurity of that life. The old ones may be regretful, but accept the inevitable with the resignation the race has always had toward any natural catastrophe. As I made my camp that night, a part of the past they still know, I wondered if we white men were not losing something as important as they, if there were any way in which we could hold on to the sense of mystery that had stirred man since his beginnings.

I sat before my fire and looked down the lake into the blue from which I had come, and as the quiet descended and the first stars came out, the coals glowed and I gazed into them as primitive men had for many thousands of years. I hoped we would never lose what I saw there, and the natives, as they learned more of their culture, would be proud of what they knew and give back to us some of the calm, serenity, and sense of belonging we have eliminated from our hurried lives on the outside.

I sincerely believe if we can somehow retain places where we can always sense the mystery of the unknown, we will find strength and beauty. In this day of strife, floundering economies, threat of war and more war, we have need of the philosophy our forebears accepted.

We often think of native tribes as being shiftless and without ambition, superstitious and ignorant. This may be true according to our point of view, but I know them well enough to realize what seems of value to us is often of no value to them. They lived with the earth and in harmony with its creatures, were part of the great silences, with no tension or hurry, perhaps cruel at times, but they learned to share and take care of each other. There was no squalor until we showed them the meaning of it. There was peace and beauty as well as suffering, starvation, and death, but these were inevitable and not to be feared.

When they gazed into their fires, as I did mine that night, they peopled the unknown with spirits both good and evil. Those glowing coals to them were full of mystery for which they had no more explanation than we had.

We know much about the universe today, the answers to many questions; we may think the mystery has gone, but that is not true. It remains and always will, for science cannot explain everything, nor begin to comprehend the meaning of love, compassion, beauty, or timelessness.

Today young natives are probing their past trying to come to grips with the meaning of ancient legends. If some find what they are looking for, they may make a contribution to the welfare of mankind greater than any progress yet achieved by us.

EVOLUTION
OF MIND

*Standing at the summit of the
ecological pyramid, man alone can
look backward billions of
years and contemplate himself.*

The most amazing thing in a universe of constant miracles is the evolution of man's mind from the same cosmic dust that produced all other forms of life. Only man has the power of perception, only he the ability to look into the future and the past, to recognize beauty and see other creatures with understanding. Man can survey the boundless universe and wonder at its meaning and what it holds for him, for he has solved the puzzle of the creation of life in the primal mists and gases of the past and finally developed a technology beyond his wildest dreams.

The fact that he has done all this from the same inanimate stellar dust as all other forms of life is the greatest miracle in nature. When man is aware of this fact alone he becomes aware of his role in a world he thinks he controls. He must never forget he holds in his own genetic complex that of all other creatures with whom he has shared the earth.

Man must recognize his past and his long struggle with

the beast within him. Without knowing where he came from, it is impossible to realize the significance of his emergence from the primeval. Scientific achievement merely opens the door to his understanding. Now that we are able to trace our evolvement physically from the first cell divisions of early forms of life to man's estate today, it is possible to understand his rise, and it is by knowing our beginnings that we comprehend the miracle.

Standing at the summit of the ecological pyramid, he alone can look backward billions of years and contemplate himself. He cannot evade his origins. If he tries, he is doomed to unhappiness and frustration. If he accepts the past as part of the divine scheme, he will know repose and balance and the illumination that comes with knowledge.

Man with such a mind has probed for meaning, has embarked on mysticism and legendry to explain the unknown. He has conjured up over the centuries the concept of an all-inclusive God, a God of reason, justice, and logic, has looked forward to the goal of attempting to create godliness in himself. The struggle for spirit has replaced the physical, and in his evolution psychologically man's greatest minds have become aware of the emptiness of material striving. The struggle has become a positive drive toward perfection, all in keeping with his final hope: realization of the kingdom of God within him.

Realizing the ultimate dream of religious consciousness, the meaning of life and man's intuitive relationship to the whole of nature gives him a goal that stands clear. Even so, the dream is still enshrouded with the mysticism that for thousands of years has clouded his knowing. If mysticism implies communion with the reality on which existence seems to rest, man may well be on the verge of knowing "the peace that passeth all understanding," and take Thomas Aquinas' advice to look at the landscape of the universe. To know great minds have been pondering the riddle for centuries and still are not sure of the meaning of truth.

When each man takes upon himself the burden of this dream, it may well be the first major step toward realization. Each must work out his own salvation, his own road to ultimate destiny. What civilization needs today is a culture of sensitivity and tolerance and an abiding love of all creatures including mankind. The future of man is the development of spirit, with love and gentleness resting in the broad field of the humanities, not in his ability to build. When he deems it his first duty to produce things for his wealth and comfort, with the end being consumption and waste, he loses dignity and purpose. The greatest thing is to be aware of what saints, sages, and philosophers have said since man first began to wonder; and, knowing what they have felt, try to see as they did. After that, the greatest thing he can do is realize he is man and to know what he has learned.

The imagination of man brings him close to the doorway of the infinite, which encompasses all. I often think of early man with his first nebulous dream as he stood at the very threshold of his rise, stirred by vague and frightening fears of the unknown.

Today he is torn by other fears, and has built around himself a civilization that cannot understand or evaluate his spiritual needs. No matter how far science has gone and will go in its exploration of the universe and of life and its processes, there are certain things it cannot do. One is to bring understanding and peace to a confused and troubled soul.

A creature of the machine age, dependent on a multiplicity of inventions most of which he does not need, is thrown into panic by a lack of energy or the denial of all that he has come to feel is essential to his way of life. Accustomed to the belief that science can cure his ills, he has reached the time when, seeing the fallacy in his dependence, he is frightened and unsure.

If he only knew a return to simplicity and harmony with the earth might be the answer, and what the sages have been saying is the truth, his burden could be easier to bear. Few, however, are capable of understanding. As Albert Schweitzer says, "Through respect for life we enter into a spiritual relationship with the world. All the efforts undertaken by philosophy, which built up grandiose systems to bring us into relation with the Absolute, have remained vain. The Absolute is so abstract in character we cannot communicate with it. It is not given to us to put ourselves at the disposal of the infinite and the inscrutable creative will, which is the basis of all existence, by having an understanding of its nature and intentions. But we enter into spiritual relationship with it by feeling ourselves under the impression of the mystery of life and devoting ourselves to all living beings whom we have the occasion and the power to serve. . . . Only that which is universal in obliging us to concern ourselves with all beings brings us truly into relationship with the Universe and the will which manifests itself in it."

And this is true regarding most people. I read this excellent essay, "On Ethics," by Schweitzer and found it comforting. In the simplicity of my cabin it was warming to have him say that the efforts of most philosophers to bring us into relationship with the Absolute are in vain, the Absolute being so abstract in character we cannot communicate with it. We are not able to put ourselves at the disposal of the infinite and the will, which is the basis of all existence. When he says we enter into a spiritual relationship with the Absolute by our feelings and searching the mystery of life, it begins to make sense. Finally his belief that only what is universal, obliging us to concern ourselves with all life, brings us truly into relationship with the universe and the will that manifests itself in wondering man.

The solution to man's probing and puzzlement is really as simple as sitting outdoors and looking at a sunset, feeding squirrels and chickadees, or caring for trees and flowers. The thought of being concerned with life is a magnificent achievement for modern man, a simple solution to his problems, which could mean peace for all who take time to know the life about them.

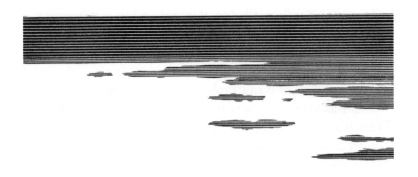

THE DREAM
OF HUDSON BAY

*If spiritual growth and maturing
of mind are what count, the dream of
fulfillment is always within reach.
The longing for Hudson Bay is behind me,
but the grandest dream of all,
entering the vast world of
comprehension and knowledge, is still alive.*

When I was young, I had a dream of someday seeing
Hudson Bay. I was a guide then, learning the intricate waterways of the Quetico-Superior country, and I used to listen to
some of the older men tell about their exploits in the vast
waters of the North. Invariably, in talking about the Albany,
the Severn, or the Gods River, they would say, "I went to the
Bay." The Bay meant only one place, Hudson Bay, and I
vowed someday I'd go there. Those stories of great wild
rivers and chains of beautiful lakes seemed almost unreal to
me, but my visions of them haunted me until at last I made it,
traversing the wide reaches of Lake Winnipeg, the Nelson,
and the Echimamish then down the historic and turbulent
Hayes, with its rapids and icy windblown lakes, to the broad
flat marshes that mark its end.

It is impossible to describe the feeling that was mine on coming out of the wilderness into the open space of the Bay. We sat in our canoes for a long time just looking at the open sea. The Bay was the only thought in my mind. No one spoke as we felt the first tidal swells; we had made it in spite of everything and my dream had been fulfilled. Strangely enough there was a certain emptiness within me, and it was a long time before its full significance dawned. In a sense I matured during that moment of realization. Now I was an old-timer and could say "I've been to the Bay."

Someone said, "Do not take from any man his dream"; when a dream is gone, hope is gone, and life can become drab and without purpose. As long as a dream is ahead, there is always something to look forward to. No doubt that was the reason for the letdown when we came to the sea, but it was not long before I knew it was only the beginning of another dream: to see the Far North rivers of the Canadian shield. Eventually I did this, and found each realization was but an open door to another adventure. I remember so well the first time I saw the famed Athabasca after coming down the Fond du lac from Reindeer and Wollaston, the Athabasca I had read about in the journals of the fur trade, a three-hundred-mile sweep to Fort Chipewyan at its far western end, the place from which the Athabasca brigades came when heading for the Churchill and Grand Portage Post.

Nor will I forget my first sight of the enormous reaches of Great Slave Lake with its countless islands, the gateway to the Coppermine River, the Thelon, and Great Bear Lake farther north; of the Great Bear River with its ninety-mile plunge to join the Mackenzie, the enormous waterway to the Arctic Sea, which the explorer Sir Alexander Mackenzie had thought was the way to the Northwest Passage and the Orient.

Those dreams are over now and I can sit in my cabin and remember as voyageurs always do, envision the entire continent, which was once open to challenge and exploration. I know a man is never so much himself as when he is actually part of a dream, never so lost as when it disappears and there is nothing to look forward to.

Every so often, communal groups attempt to find their dream in cooperative and unselfish living, with personal gain or aggrandizement sublimated to the goal of mutual need. Thoreau, Emerson, and Hawthorne were among the first, and there were countless others, but usually after a time their dreams disappeared in disillusionment. Today we have many communal groups who see such attempts as an escape from a world of strife and inequity. Many of the young have abandoned our present way of life, gone into unsettled regions of the land to build rough little cabins and live in close communion with nature and the out-of-doors.

The anachronism of this syndrome is that the majority are still dependent on the largess of parents or of those who have spent their lifetime accumulating the wherewithal to help them get started. If they are sincere in their effort to find peace in simple living, they should do as their forebears did, wrest a livelihood from the soil without help from anyone. Then and only then would they realize their dream to the fullest.

We ask, "What is the answer? How can a dream be realized, any dream?" Perhaps the answer is if a dream is seen as a perfectly created material state, it is inevitably doomed to failure. Only when it is a striving toward an attainable goal can it be achieved. In short, what is attainable is spiritual fulfillment and growth, the kind of maturing that sees and knows all, a state of being where one is in tune with ancient rhythms that give meaning to life. One can strive toward such a goal, but it takes work and patience and many years of effort. Seldom does it come to its entirety, but even so there is the deep joy of knowing one has arrived by his own efforts.

If spiritual growth and maturing of the mind are what count, the dream of fulfillment is always within reach. My dreams, like those of most people, have gone through many stages; the first was concerned mostly with physical satisfactions, finding an environment that satisfies the most simple desires—to me, vistas of beauty and meaning, the chance of knowing the great silences, and a sense of oneness with all living things. But once this is accomplished comes the search for the ultimate, which only knowledge of the earth, the universe, and man's relationship to it can bring.

This is a lifetime search and can best be begun by reading and studying the thoughts of men who since the earliest times have pondered the same identical questions. It is well to know great minds have struggled as you have to find meaning in their lives, encouraging that the vast majority reached almost identical conclusions, that only through knowledge and knowing themselves could they arrive at the answers.

The second step is the discovery of the secrets that have eluded men since the earliest days. Today, with our almost infinite understanding of nature, the whole world lies before us; but our inventive genius, while it has resulted in a multiplicity of great discoveries, is still only on the verge of knowing.

The third step is that one must realize he is not alone: most of the world is seeking peace and fulfillment, the dream going on everywhere as it always will. Each individual will interpret it in his own way and continue to strive. My own particular one goes on and on, and if I can arrive at even a glimmering of meaning and understanding of what life is all about, I shall be happy. To achieve my dream completely may be impossible; I may have to be content knowing there is some logic and reason behind the framework of the universe.

When I sit in my cabin watching the flames in my fireplace, it reminds me of countless fires I have built all over the North—but even more, I remember that mankind has gazed into fires and dreamed his dreams for centuries. The longing for Hudson Bay is behind me, and that for all other explorations I have been on, but the great dream, that of finally growing into the vast world of comprehension and knowing, is still very much alive. This is the grandest dream of all.

At last I am beginning to believe I am part of all this life and to know how I evolved from the primal dust to a creature capable of seeing beauty. This is compensation enough. No one can ever take this dream away; it will be with me until the day I have seen my last sunset, and listened for a final time to the wind whispering through the pines.

PART TWO

Search for Meaning

*The greatest achievement of our
flight to the moon is the picture
of the earth, a living blue-green
planet whirling in the dark
endless void of space, and the
realization that this is home.*

HARMONY

*Harmony is the musical
flow of environmental awareness
and evolutional knowledge
through the mind of man.*

Harmony of knowledge, will, and feeling toward the
earth is wisdom; for it has to do with living at peace with
other forms of life. At one time man lived in harmony like all
other creatures, and during most of his long existence this
had been his way of life, but today it is no longer true. Since
the beginning of civilization, harmony with nature has been
almost disregarded, though it has been recognized by a few
great minds as the only solution to the problem of finding
peace and contentment. Man has devoted his intelligence and
energy to conquering nature, subduing it, molding it to his
will. He has in the last few decades changed the surface of
the earth, crisscrossing it with a vast network of roads, excavations, and lines of communication. He has become a geological force, leveling mountains, pushing hills into valleys,
swamps, and estuaries, polluting the earth, air, and water to
the point it may soon become uninhabitable for him, as well
as all other species.

He has exhausted the earth's resources, robbed both water

and soil of nutrients, exterminated many forms of wildlife, reached a point in his savage exploitation where he must assess what he has done.

In wilderness, harmony is the natural way of life as it has always been, but we must not destroy it by overcrowding or by any exploitative use that might change it. The most important function of the wilderness for modern man is the opportunity of glimpsing for a moment what harmony really means. Having sensed it, he can bring the vision back to our urban complexes, and the wisdom that enables us to understand what we have lost. It is wisdom we are striving for in our daily lives, wisdom that colors our attitudes not only toward cities with their clamor but toward all who live within them, nearby or far removed.

My camp is tucked into a cluster of spruces and pines, with its doorway looking down a great vista of island-dotted waterway. I have just started my evening fire and a thin plume of smoke rises to the sky. The canoe is snubbed to a tree, the packs under cover, and enough kindling tucked away for morning. A squirrel chatters at me from an overhead branch and whisky jacks are already drifting in for scraps of food. It is easy to think of harmony here. The soft musical, almost ventriloquial notes of the whisky jacks—their lack of fear brings me close to them.

I eat my meal to the singing of the birds back of the tent. This to me is balance and wisdom, and I know the whole world of nature is a matter of adjustment. Harmony, I realize, is impossible to define; it is presumptive and ridiculous to say, "I am in harmony at this particular moment." Harmony is an intuitive sense, an unexplainable thing, something that is part of you without your knowing how it came about.

There are catastrophic occurrences in nature, but in time such imbalances are corrected and harmony returns. Man in his short time span, his inability to accept the long point of view, is impatient with the slowness of nature and doubtful of his world ever achieving balance. Why, he asks, do tornadoes level great stands of trees that took centuries to grow? Why do floods inundate the bottom lands of rivers, with great loss of life and destruction to countless homes, villages, and even cities? Why the ice ages that have come and gone for millions of years? Why earthquakes, wars, and disease? Why do the four horsemen of the apocalypse ride across a once peaceful earth? Why? Why? Why? Things such as these man cannot understand, for he has not the length of vision.

A year ago a sudden windstorm blew down a huge Norway pine behind my cabin. That tree had been a joy to me, but the wind came without warning, twisted it, and felled it so close to the end of the cabin that it grazed the corner and dropped its great weight next to the fireplace without harming a single other tree. When I saw it, I was shocked, knowing what could have happened, though I had been warned when a bolt of lightning hit its lofty top a couple of years ago and made a livid scar down its trunk to the ground. I knew then the tree was doomed.

I did not cut the splintered stub, but left some fifteen feet of it standing as a reminder of my good fortune. Out of the rest I made firewood, for much of it was already dead and dry. Now my woodshed has the finest kindling I could ask for and a pile of the branch ends to use in the fireplace when I want the smell of them.

I think of the spruce budworm, which has decimated millions of acres of balsam and spruce, of the cotton-boll weevil, of the blight that wiped out the great chestnut trees in the Eastern states, of the countless epidemics that have supposedly ruined forests all over the continent, and thinking about them I am sometimes sad, until I remind myself it is part of the great cycle. Though it may seem out of harmony with nature's plan, it is only because of our limited perspective that we do not comprehend.

Last summer a party of young boys camped at the north end of Basswood Lake, their tents set up on the smooth duff under a stand of big red pine. During the night, a storm blew up and a bolt of lightning hit the top of one of the tallest trees, flashed down the trunk following the root over which one of the tents was pitched, instantly killed a boy lying close to it and shocked several others. Why did it have to happen? Where was the harmony there? It was a time of sadness for the boy's parents and for his companions, and again there was no explanation. All I could think of was the old Indian tradition of never camping under big trees. Centuries of experience had taught them why.

There is more to harmony than events such as these, for it involves man's attitude toward the earth. Instead of looking at it in the concept of the old Judeo-Christian philosophy of domination—ignoring the ancient ways of nature and molding it to our wishes—we must now look at the earth with recognition of our close relationship to all life.

Our ecological crisis is simply proof we as exploiters are now reaping the results of greed and thoughtlessness, that only when we know what is meant by an ecological conscience will we ever reverse our attitude and be able to meet the situation we have created.

Harmony is evident in countless ways. It is easy to see its working in the wilds, more difficult to understand in the cities, even though there we have before us the ultimate result of our activity. We speak blithely of conservation, the environmental movement, forgetting the basis of everything is harmony. It means many things, but foremost is the realization that this old earth is our home, the only one we will ever have in spite of progress in exploring space. I often think the greatest achievement of our space effort is the picture of our beautiful blue-green planet whirling in space surrounded by an atmosphere that makes it habitable for man. More than anything coming out of these dramatic adventures, this view of the earth is the most important. For the first time man saw it with cosmic perception: this was the world he must cherish and preserve.

The astronauts who took the famous series of pictures talked about how they felt seeing all of the earth at one time, and how beautiful it was, how small and alone it appeared in the vast void of space. If all mankind could see what those men saw, the planet that had given man and all other creatures birth, if he could see at a glance the ugliness he was responsible for, if there were some way he could see the pollution of the oceans, rivers, and lakes, the swirling atmosphere around it, the mountains of garbage he has placed upon it—if this cosmic view could be extended to the point where he would realize his survival was at stake, he might be willing to do something about it.

But even though man knows, and scientists have told of the hazards we have raised, he goes his merry way, believing somehow the nightmare will go away and life continue as usual. The journeys to the moon, the explorations of Mercury and possibly other planets have demonstrated our power and ingenuity, and though there are many marvelous by-products from those efforts which add to our comfort and efficiency, unless we face reality soon, all such advances may be for naught.

Einstein's feeling for harmony puts all worries into perspective when he says: "The scientist is possessed by the sense of universal causation. . . . His religious feeling takes the form of a rapturous amazement at the harmony of natural law, which reveals an intelligence of such superiority that compared with it, all the systemic thinking and acting of human beings is an utterly insignificant reflection. This feeling is the guiding principle of his life and work. . . . It is beyond question closely akin to that which has possessed the religious geniuses of all ages."

AWARENESS

*If I knew all there is to know
about a golden arctic poppy growing
on a rocky ledge in the Far North,
I would know the whole story of
evolution and creation.*

The little bay below the cabin was calm, though white-caps were showing on the open lake in the dusk. It was autumn, the time of full color; the tall white birches and flaming maples rimming the cove glowed with the last rays of sunlight. My companion called and I hurried down to the landing. The water was translucent mother-of-pearl; the reflections so clear it was not until a slight riffle stirred the water that the birches trembled and the maples glowed anew, as though someone with a broad brush had blended them along the entire shore.

My friend, a famous photographer, turned to me and I could see his excitement. He took many pictures, caught the water when it was still and when it stirred and quivered the reflection of the trees. In his eyes were wonder and delight, and though he had spent his life portraying the beauty of many places, this for him was a perfect moment.

This sense of awareness and wonder we find in children;

teen-agers soon lose it, and adults become blasé. It is something that can be developed over the years and lost swiftly through the commonplace. It is the realization beauty is more than meets the eye, that it comes from knowledge and awareness, with time enough to look and enjoy.

I recall a canoe trip many years ago with a group of people who, for the first few days, were so involved in the affairs of the lives they had left, saw nothing and actually seemed bored. Gradually, however, boredom changed to happy acceptance of what was around them.

One of the saddest remarks anyone can make is that he is bored, just killing time, with nothing to get excited about, nothing to warrant enthusiasm. When I sense such reactions, I wonder what has happened to sights and sounds, to the senses of smell and touch, to the realization of an infinite world of beauty and mystery. Part of the answer is man has removed himself so completely from the natural scene, which used to give comfort and pleasure, his reactions have atrophied through lack of use.

Yesterday in Alaska, I snowshoed down a dog-team trail after a new snow. The tall slender spruces were stark and straight, each with a rounded cap of white. A raven soared over and, when it saw me, squawked loudly. I could still see color in the Labrador tea, the faded bronzes and yellow brown of grasses, fireweed stalks covered with dusted fuzz; in a hidden spot beneath a protecting stump, a cluster of Linnaea leaves and knew where I could look in the spring. Though far from home, I did not feel strange, for all these things except the mountains were merely an extension of the Quetico-Superior country thousands of miles away.

I climbed a gradual slope, left the spruce behind, and went through a forest of birch, their slender branches bent low under their load. Then I burst through the cover at the top of another ridge, and before me were the mighty jagged peaks of the Chugach Range. It was as though I had stepped through a door. Forgotten now were the little things: the stitching of mouse tracks; a weasel's delicate imprint on the surface, then disappearing, investigating every hummock; a fox track running down the trail ahead; the spruces full of chickadees, red polls, and siskins, the seeds and bracts from their feeding scattered over the snow. All these were forgotten in the magnificent vista of mountains dominating everything.

Framing the view before me were two tall spruces, and I took several pictures so I would remember. It was getting late, the sun sinking fast, when I caught the first tinge of alpenglow toward the west, a glow that spread swiftly over the range to the east. The same brush that stirred the waters of my little bay at home was now stroking the snowy peaks until the entire complex of pinnacles, valleys, and cirques was tinged with rose. For just a moment the color held, then faded quickly in the northwest, leaving the mountains gray and cold.

Awareness is becoming acquainted with environment, no matter where one happens to be. Man does not suddenly become aware or infused with wonder; it is something we are born with. No child need be told its secret; he keeps it until the influence of gadgetry and the indifference of teen-age satiation extinguish its intuitive joy.

Being with children who do not know the why or wherefore of life is a joy: wonder and excitement are always there. It can be nurtured and actually enhanced, but one must never allow knowledge to destroy its primitive delight.

Often I think of a professor of mine, a great naturalist and one of the pioneers of our present concepts of plant and animal ecology, who usually forgot the names of plants, insects, and birds we encountered on our various field trips. One day, puzzled at his lack of knowledge, I asked why he did not know the names, and I shall never forget his answer: "I am more interested in broad ecological concepts. I can hire dozens of smart taxonomists who are encyclopedias of the names of living creatures. When I need them, I call, but I cannot clutter my mind with unessentials. It is enough to know how living things fit into the great scheme of interrelationships." Too much attention to scientific detail can rob one of awareness and deeper meanings.

Another point worth remembering is the way these interrelationships work, how intricately they are woven into the fabric of the whole, including how living things became what they are. The new science of microbiotics is a good example, the growing understanding of viruses, molds, and bacteria, not to mention the infinite complexities of a tiny flower. Again one must be simple in explanation, not making it so complex that it might destroy the very thing one is trying to teach. This in itself takes knowledge, and only when it is thoroughly understood can it be imparted to others. With this understanding, awareness can grow from the appreciation of color, form, and movement to the great secrets of relationship. After a lifetime of studying the sciences and keeping abreast of recent discoveries, I find myself capable of more and more excitement at what I see. Even an adult can grow in perception if he refuses to close the doors to learning.

"Killing time"—I often think of the expression and how swiftly time passes in the out-of-doors where there is never a moment without something new: dawns and sunrises with mists moving out of the bays, the shifting of clouds, the way light plays with water and trees, the sound of bird calls, the sight of flowers, the movement of animals, the magic of dusk and the last slanting rays of color.

Being windbound in the lee behind a rocky gale-swept point, knowing one cannot move for hours or days, might seem to some an instance of "killing time," but to me it is always an opportunity. I recall such an occasion north of Great Slave Lake. The vistas were new across the storm-tossed open water, and from a protecting ledge I watched great battalions of whitecaps shining in the sun. I leaned against the wind and shivered with cold, then climbed down to our sheltered campsite to survey its possibilities: a fireplace close to the water, a level spot between two ragged trees tortured by the winds of many years. They were trees of timberline, of gales and snows, and though no more than a few inches in diameter, I know they were over a hundred years of age, so hard and tough it would be almost impossible to chop one down if it were dead and dry. I rubbed some of the branch ends in my hand and reveled in the strong resinous odor. Their roots went down into a cleft of the ledge, the secret of their long survival. They could not be uprooted no matter how savagely the wind tore at them.

I found two arctic poppies, yellow as gold; if we had not stopped, we would have missed them, one dab of color on a barren shore. This simple flower so typical of the North is always a cause for wonder, as all flowers are. If I knew all there is to know about this simple poppy, I would know the whole story of evolution and creation. I remember the Bible verses:

Consider the lilies of the field, how they grow;
they toil not, neither do they spin:
And yet I say unto you, That even Solomon in all
his glory was not arrayed like one of these.

I always treasure any place where I have been windbound and, looking back, have never regretted one, no matter how long such enforced interludes might threaten the distances ahead and the schedule of travel. There is no such thing as killing time, for time is enhanced by the gift of solitude.

We think we are finding all the answers, but this can never be done, for there are certain things that cannot be explained: relationships, intuitions, the grand thrust of the evolutional process, the riddle of a bloodstream, nuclear and genetic knowledge, the life-giving function of chloroplasts. The longer I contemplate this world of living things and look at the earth itself, the more I am convinced there can never be an end to wonder and awareness, and that one of the real tragedies in life is to waste time when there is so much to see and learn.

ALIVENESS

*The bronzed Tahitian with a strand
of seaweed around his hair was grace
and poetry personified as his surfboard
topped a combing crest. His was a sense
of aliveness and intensity most of us
seldom know.*

An old-timer once told me some people are dead before
they are born; take life so seriously they find no joy in anything about them. I've often thought of that, and, watching
men and their reactions in the woods, I have found many full
of joy and excitement, others as grim and unsmiling as those
my friend had encountered.

Since we go through this strange and beautiful world of
ours only once, it seems a pity to lack the sense of delight and
enthusiasm that merely being alive should hold. Perhaps for
the dour ones it is lack of knowledge, a feeling of being
surfeited and replete, needing nothing to look forward to, but
I think it goes deeper than this: a genetic quality, perhaps, of
fear, desperation, and hopelessness from a race of unfortu-
nate survivors.

I have reached the conclusion that enthusiasm and aliveness may be inborn, an intuitive understanding that comes

from the amazing miracle of life itself. The fortunate ones have this subconscious inspiration and do not have to be taught the meaning of enthusiasm. They know what a privilege it is to have senses that are responsive in every way aliveness can be interpreted.

It is a pleasure to be with people of this type. My son Sig and his wife, Esther, of Alaska belong! Any trip with them—whether on skis, snowshoes, by canoe, or on foot—is an adventure. Esther once said to me, "Do you know what makes me more excited than anything else? It's the smell of wet earth in the spring or fall, the rich dampness of the earth itself"—a primal sort of thing with her, so deep it encompasses everything.

Young Sig and I made a moonlight trek through the muskeg one evening two months ago when the west was still aglow with the sunset. Though he had made countless trips during his many years in this part of the North, he was entranced with the new snow clinging to the thin spires of the spruces, the laden birches drooping and glistening; it was almost as though this were his first experience. We stopped where the trail crosses Campbell Creek and listened to the soft purring of open water on its way to the sea. "Following the spring breakup, Dolly Vardens, some rainbow, and even salmon will be up," he said. When we got home from our little foray, his eyes were glowing.

It is true one is more alive when confronted by danger, with faculties surcharged and senses sharpened to their finest edge, but excitement and aliveness do not have to depend on peril to make themselves known. They rely more on the simple ability to feel deeply.

There are those who, even though they respond inwardly, say nothing, show no outward sign whatever. One would think they were not alive, but I have found reticence is no indication of lack of feeling. Sometimes those who feel and do not show it may actually be more alive than those who do. To them nothing is more disturbing than to live constantly on the crest of an emotional wave of excitement and enthusiasm. Indians seldom talk about their emotions, but the feeling is there, so much a part of what is around them, they do not have to show it, and would feel uncomfortable with those who did.

Coleridge said, "Only in ourselves does nature live"— meaning perhaps that the joy we know in nature is older and more profound than any other known to man. Loren Eiseley, speaking of the lonely ones who frequently show nothing, made much the same implication when he said "they may leave a noisy crowded room to stare with relief into the abyss of space."

Perhaps it is eagerness that expresses the idea of enthusiasm and aliveness as well as any, the eagerness to know and feel, and I agree with Lewis Mumford that without at least some consciousness of the beauty of life in all its great variety, some intensity and quickening of rhythm, music, or laughter, humanity is not safe.

Intensity may be what we are talking about in trying to understand aliveness, for without it there can be no quickening of the spirit. I never think of intensity without remembering a fisherman I knew. Fishing to him was far more than catching fish; he became so intensely alive in his concentration nothing else counted; he neither spoke nor laughed, and nothing in the world could have distracted him. The loons might cavort beside the canoe, a moose emerge from the shoreline, but the only thing that could have possibly made him swerve the slightest from what he was doing was if the moose swam toward the canoe. Even then I am sure he would only have been annoyed, not frightened. He was the epitome of aliveness, intensity, and eagerness.

It was the same when he was hunting ducks. He would stand by the hour scanning the sky, not a wing or a movement in the heavens, but the intensity was there, and should something actually come over, it paid off, for all his faculties were attuned to what he must do—line up his bird, lead it properly with carefully calculated wind and speed. I recall one high shot he made—far too high, it seemed to me—but I knew what was going through his mind and the ultimate result when that bird folded its wings and lit before him in a pillar of spray. There should have been a shout of joy, some sign of triumph or a smile of satisfaction, but he was one of the silent ones and nothing ever showed.

When brook-trout fishing, he would stand in one spot with unbelievable patience, watching the rising of a fish, the slow circling of ripples spreading toward him, the movement of insects on the water. I could swear he knew what that trout was thinking, and at the moment was perhaps more trout than man. The only way I could explain this old friend was that in him was a heritage of countless centuries of the hunter and fisherman when a man actually became the quarry he sought. Through genetics and environment, this was a combination of all aliveness implied. If he had been a hunter of the old nomadic days, he would have been a hero to his tribe, one of the great ones, a legend of his time. He did not have to tell me he was enjoying himself, nor laugh and sing and jump around and pound me on the back; I knew him too well for that.

In my early days I was a good skier, or thought I was, and to me no joy was as great as when there was powder snow on a firm base, usually during the month of March, when one could career down hills and take slopes that ordinarily would have been impossible. I have discovered today I know nothing about skiing with modern equipment, and have watched skiers come down mountain slopes almost flying and lost in a blinding flurry of snow, but from my own experience I know their feeling and can sense their joy as they race down some suicidal slope.

I have the same sensation when among surfers who pursue the big waves all over the world, especially off Waikiki in Hawaii: the suspense of waiting for the big swell that always comes, the swift paddling to get in line with its force, then the supreme moment when the lift of it hurls you toward a beach half a mile away. Excitement is there, eagerness, and joy. I'll never forget a bronzed Tahitian boy with a strand of seaweed tied around his flowing black hair, his grace as he all but flew on a combing crest. His was a sense of being alive with an intensity most humans seldom know.

I've known it running rapids on Northern rivers, being committed and maneuvering swiftly from one smooth slick to another, watching the standing waves, keeping away from rocks and ledges that could destroy you, and when it is all over, with the violence and roar of water behind, turning for one more look of triumph before moving on toward the next challenge.

I cannot begin to enumerate the many kinds of aliveness one may know, for each individual has different needs. For me there is the thrill of some writing well done—after hours and perhaps days of searching and probing, of finding the correct word or phrase that says exactly what I wanted to say, the moment when for some strange and unexplainable reason I hear at last a certain melody that has haunted me.

ONENESS

*The dog team belonged to the
Far North as much as the howling
of huskies around native villages
when northern lights swirled,
as much a part of the old Alaska as
the endless vistas of space and wildness.*

Oneness is a sense of communion vital to man's mental well-being and to his survival. It does not come just by being called upon; it is a constant feeling, far more than a point of view, a permanent attitude that colors all we do. In the tundra of the Far North I felt at home as I watched a herd of caribou weaving its way through the taiga. The ground was rich with hues of cranberries, dwarf birches, cloudberries, and withered flowers.

Oneness recognizes all things, the harsh with the benevolent, the cruel with the kind, violence with peace—all of it belonging to those who know it. Oneness can be felt anywhere on a city street, in a quiet pool, at home, or on some raging ocean coast. It does away with fear.

This morning while snowshoeing down a dog-team trail north of Anchorage, a moose kept pace with me moving slowly and unafraid through the scrub birch and alder. The huge animal stopped under a down tree and munched the branch ends contentedly. It was sleek and fat, for there were no enemies, no wolves to harry him—only man, and the hunting season was over for the year.

I crossed a creek and watched the flow under the snowbanks, followed the old trail onto an open meadow crisscrossed with fresh moose tracks. The animals were hidden from sight, no doubt feeding in the jungle of willow and alder around it. I looked at the thin spires of spruce, toward the uplands where the trees were larger, and told myself: here is most of Alaska as far north as the Brooks Range, endless miles of muskeg threaded with little creeks, range after range of mountains, the foothills reaching in a ragged fringe of sparser and sparser growth until at last there is only snow. Each peak, I knew, was separated from the other by valleys, the passes for travel. This was the old North, almost a thousand miles of it reaching as far as the Bering Sea beyond the great North Slope.

This was the Alaska I knew before the great oil boom, and it was hard to realize from Valdez to Fairbanks and through the forbidding Brooks Range the bulldozers, tractors, and diesels were changing the land forever with corridors, roads, pipe and gas lines, a boom that would have far greater impact than the gold rush of 1898. Gold changed the Yukon and the Klondike, and thousands of men came to know the North for the first time. Those scars are mostly gone after some seventy-five years, but the greater scars of the pipelines and roads will not disappear for thousands of years. The land is crawling with workers from the lower forty-eight, men who, like those of the gold rush, are there to make a fortune. Some will stay, some fall in love with the country as the pioneers did almost a century ago, but the land will never be the same, for the old sense of belonging and oneness will be gone.

For me the old feeling was still there, the same I had found in the Northwest Territories and in the wilderness of the Quetico-Superior. That would never leave, for it was part of my blood and sinew; it had already seeped into the deeper pool of my consciousness. Oneness and harmony are the same, in a sense, but oneness is deeper, more psychological. Much has been written about it, but few can explain.

Environmental centers springing up across the land have as a major tenet teaching oneness with the earth, but some who teach often do not understand it themselves and cannot impart it to others. I sometimes think the best way to teach is through example. If an individual can personify this feeling by living and doing, it may rub off by personal contact.

I am often asked to speak to environmental groups, to take them on field trips, and to instill a sense of awareness and oneness; I sometimes wonder how successful I am. It is gratifying to receive letters telling me they did get the feeling of belonging. There are many young people today who are very aware of this whole problem, whose sensitivity is so deeply felt they may be able to share it with others. These young are steeped in the psychology of mental processes, many with background in the natural sciences. Never before has there been such a nationwide urge among people to devote their lives to the important field of environmental understanding. Perhaps in time they will know the answers far better than I.

Last night it was bright moonlight and the temperature twenty below when my son and I hiked down the same dog-team trail to enjoy the moon shining on the birches and expanses of muskeg. He did not have to call my attention to the scene any more than I did his, so we walked along without comment. We have made many trips together since his boyhood, when we used to dash off on some expedition without preparation or forethought, with a sense of adventure and being at one with the land that guided us, a communion beyond the need for words.

On the way back from our hike we heard a dog team, saw it coming toward us, and stepped off into the deep snow to let it pass: a beautiful team of Siberians training for races coming up, possibly even the big one—the Iditarod, a thousand miles from Anchorage to Nome. The driver laughed as he passed, waved in appreciation of our having given way, then disappeared behind us. He and his team belonged to the whole Alaska scene, were one with the country. The joyousness of such travel has always impressed me. Of course there were times when the going was hard, the feet of dogs cut and bleeding from broken ice, temperatures at forty or fifty below that took the heart out of them, and it became a matter of survival to keep moving; days when the driver had to break trail for the dogs, making a few hundred yards at a time; but those times are forgotten when the going is good and all is well.

Oneness—that driver and his dogs had it, and if asked to explain, it would be as impossible for him to do so as for me. The very sight of them was enough. They have always been part of the Far North, as much a part as the howling of huskies around the villages when northern lights swirl and play in a shifting panorama of color, part of endless vistas and the sense of space and wildness.

BEAUTY

Beauty never stands alone,
is so fragile it can be destroyed by
a sound or a foreign thought. It may
be infinitesimally small or encompass
the universe itself.

In nature all things are beautiful. An old professor of mine, a renowned botanist, once told me he could see as much beauty in a patch of tundra or a lichen-covered rock as he could in a grove of majestic sequoias, that all living things are beautiful if one realizes what has gone into their evolution. The mysteries of how plants live and gain their sustenance, their adaptations to environment, the infinite interdependencies between them and all living things make each one a miracle in itself.

Beauty is composed of many things and never stands alone. It is part of horizons, blue in the distance, great primeval silences, knowledge of all things of the earth. It embodies the hopes and dreams of those who have gone before, including the spirit world; it is so fragile it can be destroyed by a sound or thought. It may be infinitesimally small or encompass the universe itself. It comes in a swift conception wherever nature has not been disturbed.

John Galsworthy said: "It is the contemplation of beautiful visions which slowly, generation by generation, has lifted man to his present state. Nothing in the world but the love of beauty in its broadest sense stands between man and the full and reckless exercise of his competitive greed."

Julian Huxley said that the important ends of man's life include: the creation and enjoyment of beauty, both natural and man-made, that increases comprehension and provides a more assured sense of significance; the preservation of all sources of pure wonder, such as fine scenery, wild animals in freedom, unspoiled nature; the attainment of inner peace and harmony; the feeling of active participation in embracing enduring projects, including the project of evolution.

There is beauty everywhere if one can see and understand its meaning. Someone said, "Beauty is in the eye of the beholder," and this no doubt is true, for no two people see anything alike. We know, however, it has a strange power of giving peace and joy, and through the ages has been one of the most powerful creative thrusts. Its very existence is tangible proof of the spirit and man's ability beyond that of all other creatures to perceive it.

I never watch a sunset without feeling the scene before me is more beautiful than any painting could possibly be, for it has the additional advantage of constant change, is never the same from one instant to the next. When one considers the sound effects that go with it in the North, the calling loons, the whisper of wings overhead, their silhouettes against the glow, the scene has such significance it is hard to leave until dark comes and the west, with the iridescence of waters, has changed to the black of night. Nothing can equal this.

Swamps are particularly beautiful to me, for in them, I know, is true wilderness. I like them in the spring when they

are alive with red-winged blackbirds, with their merry
"conkoree" from perches on the dead stalks of cattails, and
when black ducks explode around every bend in a wild confusion as they climb toward the sky. I appreciate them in the
fall when heathers become coppery and even the sphagnum is
full of color, and the pitcher plants stand bold and tall as they
change from summer's green to red. Dwarf birches and sweet
gale have by then followed suit and with the gold of rushes
make the bog an unforgettable delight.

Flowers always give me joy: the sky-blue hepatica against
the brown of last year's leaves, the almost hidden pink and
white of arbutus along some portage trail, fireweed with its
flaming masses after a burn, Indian paintbrush against a gray
rock, crimson woodbine twined around gray weathered
stumps, a drift of pink Linnaea under the pines after the
snows of winter, a carpet of yellow cowslips beside a tiny
rivulet, the miracle of pine trees in full bloom, the tiny
crimson flowers of hazel at the tips of branches still without
leaves. All of them give me pleasure, and knowing the long
evolution of their formation makes their beauty even more
significant.

There are so many things to see—the beauty of a storm
with a dark bank of cloud split into fragments by flashes of
lightning, the eerie unreal light, the roll of thunder, the waiting for the deluge, and the silence after it has passed.

There are crashing waves at dusk or whitecaps in morning, sunlight marching across the open spaces challenging my
canoe.

Moonlight has beauty through a stand of pines, the long
path of it across a lake or river, on a pool of a trout stream,
or on the snow of a ski trail with the black shadows of trees
and the wintry silences. Toward April there are rosy purplish
tints of birches—warming-up colors, I call them, getting ready

for spring. Winter has beauty in stillness when the skies are spangled with stars and the northern lights shimmer across the horizon.

Many kinds of beauty manifest themselves, and I sometimes feel animals in their movements when they are undisturbed top the list: the undulating flow of a mink along the water's edge, the sinuous swimming of an otter, the graceful leap of a deer clearing a windfall, the flowing loose-jointed gait of a running wolf over the ice of a frozen river, even the smooth movement of a great ungainly moose through the thickest cover along a lakeshore.

One of the most beautiful creations in nature is the brook trout, *Salvelinus fontinalis,* taken from a spring-fed stream: the beauty of its coloring—the mottling of black and green, its glowing red spots, the orange stripes along the creamy underside and tips of fins—the quivering aliveness as it comes out of the water. I have often said a brook trout is far too beautiful and gorgeously arrayed to eat. To watch one take a fly is a picture of beauty in action, one of the miracles in the world of wilderness movement.

It is birds I watch, perhaps, more than any other—the soaring of ravens, ospreys, and eagles high in the blue, their effortless drifting and grace in the wind currents over the earth below. The amazing flight of hummingbirds as they hover near the corollas of some flower, their ability to fly forward with a lightning thrust for nectar and then reverse and disappear in a line as straight and purposeful as the flight of a bee.

There is beauty in sound, the howling of wolves and the harmony that comes when a pack is in full cry, the same kind of music I have heard when loons call together and answer their echoes from distant lakes. Experts say the calling of birds is to protect territory, but I wonder if this is true. Why should purple finches sing long after the nesting season is over? Why the clarion call of bluejays in the fall, why the howling dogs around Indian and Eskimo villages when the moon is full? Who is to say these sounds are not enjoyed by them as much as we enjoy the songs we sing? Are we the only creatures so endowed? I firmly believe, though they may not have our perception, they make music for the pure thrill of it.

The other night I listened to the howling of a timber wolf, at first long eerie full-throated calls and short doglike barkings, then the answering of others far away, and at last what I had been waiting for, a chorus of indescribable harmony and blending of tones. While there may not have been more than five or six, it sounded as though there were forty, a wilderness chorus that always thrills me.

Loons do exactly the same, a few introductory long calls or laughing cadences, then the cadenza of many. So it is with hermit thrushes, a single call or two until there are enough birds responding to make it sound as though the aspen were alive with song.

All of us have special places of great beauty. One of my favorites at sunset in the winter is looking across a barren hillside with a rim of birches silhouetted against its color. It has always fascinated me and I have often wished I could paint that delicate tracery against the reddening sky. Another is a high ridge that commands a view of many miles to the east. To see a moonrise there, to watch a certain notch begin to brighten and finally see the golden rim slip above the dark horizon never fails to fill me with awe and wonderment.

In a lifetime of seeing beauty in the wilderness, I always feel a lift of spirit and an afterglow of serenity and content. I also know one must take time and wait for the glimpses of beauty that always come, and one must see each as though it were his last chance.

Of all creatures, we have the power to appreciate beauty and are able to contemplate its meaning. Man has come from the same earth stuff as other creatures, but through the accident of evolutional development we are the fortunate ones. But again I wonder if we alone have this power of appreciation. Is it not possible other creatures feel more than we think? They may not be able to analyze, but there might be some genetic quality, which makes them conscious of color, sound, and movement, that inspires them as it does us.

I think of the screaming of terns over the marshes and lakes of the Far North, of the curlews' lonely cries on the tundra, and if I let my imagination run, I seem to catch something beyond the physical, which blends with my own exaltation.

But why the joy and inspiration of beauty at all? Why should it have the impact it does? This I cannot answer, but I do know ugliness brings revulsion, aggression, hate, and even anger, while beauty always gives joy and a sense of fulfillment.

SIMPLICITY

*Simplicity in all things is one
of the secrets of the wilderness.*

Thoreau advised us to "drive life into a corner and reduce it to its simplest terms," recognizing the truth that complexity robs us of time and energy by making life so involved with the unessential, the real things are forgotten and never seen. In the wilds, on any expedition, it takes time to settle down and forget unimportant distractions and concepts. It is only when the shakedown comes, as we say in the North, that one begins to feel free.

As I mentioned in my book *The Lonely Land,* when we approached our first campsite on Ile-à-la-Crosse, it seemed as though we had never been away from it. Strange how swiftly one moves into a wilderness way of life, how airplane terminals, crowds, and cities, even jobs, move into the background and seem secondary compared to being under way and on one's own. We had a campsite to find and whip the outfit into shape before dark. This is it, I told myself, this the way to Athabasca, Great Slave, and the Mackenzie, country which had haunted my dreams for years.

The important thing with my voyageurs was the fact our shakedown had taken place long ago; duties were simple, and supplies and equipment stripped to the bone. With less experienced travelers in the bush, it is different; the problem of sorting out unnecessary food and clothing, and things one does not need.

Life is complicated at best, and those who never break away from normal involvements to the simplicities of wilderness travel cannot know what they are missing, nor what is meant by unlimited time or unlimited room, the privilege of looking at the old familiar world without interruption.

In a city we are saturated with a multitude of gadgets we have been urged to buy through the blandishments of advertising, most of which are of no consequence to happiness or welfare. With the so-called crunch now upon us, we have discovered we can reduce our energy consumption and do without many things we thought were essential.

The hallmark of the affluent society has been to use and discard. For generations it has been an accepted belief, and now for the first time, looking back at those days of lacking nothing, we find we can live without overheated homes, electric toothbrushes, blenders, and electric blankets, that even the mellow glow of candlelight is something to enjoy. To me this is the great plus of the present crisis, and I believe our people will think twice before they succumb again to superfluity and waste.

On pack and canoe trips today I look askance at the many freeze-dried foods we take along. They are wonderful in a way, but the variety makes us plan menus as though a shopping center were around every corner—not to mention what must be taken along to prepare them.

I think of my own travels: breakfasts were usually porridge with a cup of tea and some dried milk and sugar. Seldom do I carry luxuries such as bacon, ham, or sausage. Porridge with dried fruit or native fruit, if wild berries are ripe, is enough. Lunch is always just a snack: hard dried meat or jerky or a sliver of cheese or hard sausage with hardtack, and powdered juice for drinking, or on a cold wet day, a pot of tea or dried soup. The evening meal should also be plain. I am a great believer in stews, fish chowder with flour turned into it to give it body, a sprinkling of dried onions or potatoes, and a little salt and pepper for flavor. If you do not have fish, pemmican or dried meat will do, and of course there is always bannock or frying-pan bread with berries stirred into the batter.

Many old-timers eat only two meals a day, as the Indians and voyageurs did. After starting early in the morning, they made a stop about midday for a combination breakfast and snack, and again when camp was pitched at night, but always something simple. There are foods which do not have to be freeze-dried or precooked, such as rice, beans, peas, and dried fruit. Of course if one really wants to splurge, a tin of butter or jam adds much to any meal, but the point is we can go without much of the fancy food now taken as a matter of course. Simplicity is all-essential and we can get used to basic foods with little effort. When traveling in the bush, one's appetite is great enough to make even the most rudimentary diet delicious.

During my guiding days, one of the most disagreeable tasks was telling men of any party what they must leave behind. For a short trip of ten days or two weeks, one pair of boots, a single pair of snagproof pants, two pairs of wool socks, a wool shirt, and a sweater with a rainproof windbreaker are enough anywhere in the near North, and one very important item is an old serviceable hat to keep the sun, as well as rain, out of one's eyes. I have gone on many long trips with only this equipment. Somehow it never occurs to people they can wash clothes enroute, mend them if necessary;

and if you do not want your shirt to get wet in a rainstorm, you can strip to the buff without harm. Skin will dry, and after the rain is over, one can again don the shirt or sweater. The same applies to fishing tackle. A good casting rod or a fly rod is enough, with not more than half a dozen baits or flies. An old friend of mine, Dr. Preston Bradley of Chicago, a great bass fisherman, never took more than a dozen flies, all of one type, the Ambrose Bucktail, for he discovered he could take all the fish he needed with that fly alone. Once I guided an outdoor writer, Bob Becker of the Chicago *Tribune*. Bob had a huge box of every conceivable fly or lure, plus several rods. All I had were a few flies tucked into the band of my hat and an old beaten-up Heddon rod, which had been on many trips. After we had been out a couple of days, Bob finally asked me the question I had been expecting. "You're supposed to be the authority on fly-fishing in this country," he said; "where's your outfit?"

"This is all of it," I said, tossing him my hat and pointing to my old rod and single-action reel. Then I fished an extra leader out of my wallet to show him I was not too impoverished.

Another time I guided the tackle manufacturer Charley Heddon, who literally had a trunkful of lures he felt he must try out. This I could understand, for fishing tackle was his business, but with my simple outfit I did as well as he. I never think of such fishing equipment without remembering another old friend, Buck Sletton, a fellow guide in the early days. Someone in his party could not make up his mind what kind of lures to buy even though Buck had told him. Finally in exasperation he said, "Mister, are you buying those lures for yourself or for the fish?"

Simplicity in all things is the secret of the wilderness and one of its most valuable lessons. It is what we leave behind that is important. I think the matter of simplicity goes further than just food, equipment, and unnecessary gadgets; it goes into the matter of thoughts and objectives as well. When in the wilds, we must not carry our problems with us or the joy is lost. Never indulge in arguments or bitter recriminations; never criticize, but be of good cheer. I like the quote from the diary of Father Le Jeune to young Jesuit missionaries attached to the fur brigades of almost a hundred and fifty years ago (1830):

"You should be prompt in embarking and disembarking. Do not carry either water or sand into the canoe. It is not wise to ask too many questions, nor should you yield to the itch for making comments about the journey, a habit which may be cultivated to an excess. Silence is a safe and discreet plenishing. Should there be need of criticism, let it be conducted modestly.

"In brief, it is well to be cheerful, or at any rate to appear so. Everyone at a portage should try to carry something according to his strength, be it only a kettle. For example, do not begin paddling if you are not to continue paddling. Stick to your place in the canoe. Be assured if once you are set down as a troublemaker and a difficult person, you will not easily get rid of such a reputation."

His advice would hold today on any wilderness trip: keep your thoughts simple; do not be argumentative or meddlesome. Do not hate, condemn, or criticize; an expedition is too short for that, as is life. Learn to live simply and all will go well.

Thoreau, I know, would have agreed with Buck, and even with me, and I can imagine him moving around the old Wilderness Outfitters warehouse with his strange and almost enigmatic smile, patting the guides on the shoulder and whispering, "Simplify—simplify—simplify."

COURAGE

*Sisu—you could see it in the eyes
of the people, that indomitable courage
which meant they would rather die than
submit. You find it in all who have
lived with danger, that quality which
makes a people unconquerable.*

Courage is a many-faceted virtue. There is physical courage and the courage of conviction and belief. There is courage to withstand suffering without complaint, to show calmness and humility in the face of success and adulation; but above all, there is the courage of withstanding adversity of all kinds, with what our Finnish people call *sisu*, an inner strength and indomitable persistence which never admits defeat. All types are closely intertwined, all of the same cloth.

Most think of courage in terms of the physical, being willing to face certain death with calmness or injury, without thought of self. I recall vividly, when I was a boy in a small town, watching a runaway team of horses tearing along out of control; the wagon reeled from side to side, its occupants a woman with several children.

People stood transfixed with horror, but then a man dashed out, caught the bridle of the nearest horse, and, in spite of wildly flailing hoofs, brought the team to a stop just before it careened off the street into a rocky gorge. The scene made a tremendous impression on me, and I've never forgotten it. Call it true grit, courage, bravery, or whatever you will, it proved a man can risk his life for others, and in the last analysis that is what counts.

It taught me another lesson: one cannot run from a challenge without losing. To flee is signing a death warrant to dignity and character, and, having run, there is no return; one is a weakling forever. Meeting a challenge, though one may be defeated, gives strength, character, and a certain assurance that regardless of outcome, one will survive or go down fighting. It is much like running a rapids: as you approach the dropoff where water quickens slightly, and there is still time to swerve away to safety, you have the barest intimation of what may be ahead. Let us call it apprehension, but as the current grows faster and faster and there is no retreat, you know you must go through, come what may. It takes courage from then on, something involved with hormones that surges from deep inside, and a certain recklessness that places you on the crest of a wave, the thrill that always comes with danger.

Once, returning from a trip in the Far North, I flew south to Edmonton. A young boy came into the plane and sat beside me; apparently he had just taken part in one of the rodeos, for he was still in his riding outfit, Western hat, high-heeled cowboy boots, worn Levis, and he carried a pair of leather chaps on his arm. He looked about seventeen or eighteen, and when I asked his name, he told me and added that he'd been riding for ten years on the Calgary circuit and was on his way to Denver for another ride at the rodeo there.

"Ever get scared?" I asked him. He laughed. "Mister," he

said, "I'm scared half the time. When you stand beside the chute and your bronc comes down, you take one look. If his eyes are blue, that's bad; if it's got a Roman nose and a loose lower lip, that's bad, too. Right then I'm scared, but I climb on just the same, and all of a sudden we're out of the chute going like the wind. If I can stay on the first jump or two, I'm all right and might ride the critter to the end. Not scared any more after that first wild jump.

"What do you do, Mister?" he asked.

"Well," I said, "I've been riding canoes up North down some of those rivers a thousand miles or more from here."

"That sounds real dangerous," he said. "I wouldn't like to do that. Ever scared?"

"Yes," I admitted. "I'm just as scared as you are waiting for your horse to come down. When I'm at the top of a bit of wild water and know I've got to go through, I'm scared stiff until I get into it; then I feel as you do and can ride anything that comes."

"I still wouldn't like it," he said. "You must be crazier than I am."

I left him at Seattle, wished him luck, felt his hard hand for a moment, and caught the glint of understanding in his blue eyes. He knew and I knew, and there was nothing more to be said. As I worked my way down the aisle of the plane, I thought of the great geologist Sir Richard Camsell, who had helped plan our trip up the Camsell River to Great Bear, and his answer to the question I had put to him. "After the thousands of miles you've traveled in the North," I said, "the countless rapids you've run, have you ever been really scared?"

He smiled. "Scared? I'm scared every time I run a rapids —you never can tell what will happen—but it's fear laced with exhilaration."

That is what is behind most cases of physical courage. There is always a sense of fear, but the reward is one of added awareness and joy at having come through. This is what motivates all who risk their lives: mountain climbers, white-water men, broncobusters, automobile or speedboat racers, or those who go to the sea in ships, sails full of the wind, with only knowledge, skill, and courage to carry them through.

There is a different kind of courage, too, that of conviction and belief, the willingness to stand up and be counted before one's enemies. If one has it and fails to face ridicule when the battle lines are drawn, then one is a coward. It is as courageous to take criticism and scorn with equanimity as to withstand a physical threat. History is full of men who are remembered for their unswerving convictions, their faith in God or belief in eternal values. The weaklings are forgotten, or live on in infamy. Though courage has meant death, torture, or persecution to many, it has added steel to the human spirit and the hardiness not to falter when facing danger.

Sisu, from the Finnish, encompasses not only the various aspects of courage, but something deeper, a combination of qualities so deeply inbred into a people's psyche it is difficult even for them to explain. In 1945, I visited a Finn who had been through the desperate winter war against the Russians. It was just after the close of World War II while the big guns across the bay from Helsinki threatened the city with instant destruction should its ancient enemies decide the time for complete submission and invasion had come.

"How can you stand the threat of those guns," I asked him, "knowing that any day might be your last? How can you laugh and sing and go about your work with this diabolical threat hanging over you?"

His answer was simple. "We have learned to live with it," he replied. "Life must go on. In time it will be different, and of course there is this matter of *sisu*."

Sisu—you could see it in the eyes of the people, that indomitable courage which meant they would die rather than submit. Dignity, pride, refusal to accept defeat—you find it in all people who have lived with danger, the one great human quality that makes a man human or a people unconquerable.

My little Finnish sauna down in the bay, built as saunas always have been, rich with the smells of countless fires, cedar and birch, epitomizes *sisu* and the ultimate peace it brings. As I said in *Runes of the North*:

> After the last steaming, we returned to the lake for a final dip. The setting sun was tinting the water, the west pink and blue with a broad band of color in the bay. We swam through it, lay in its iridescence, looking back toward the sauna in the cedars. Though the fire was almost gone, smoke still rose from the chimney, and we could smell it there on the water.
>
> Back on the little dock we sat and cooled ourselves. A sudden breeze fluttered the aspen leaves far above and we could hear the soft rushing of the river a mile away. There was nothing of moment to talk about; ours was a sense of fullness and belonging to a past of simple ways. Venus hung like a great lamp in the darkening sky. This was a time of magic when the world was still here, the feel of dawns and awakenings at night, of hush and quiet and open space.

This, I thought, is what the Finns fought for, what gave them *sisu*, the feel of a home worth dying for—at the heart of it love of the earth with all its challenges and rewards.

It is what gives environmentalists the strength to battle for the land they love, to take scorn and epithets in their stride, knowing they are fighting for something eternal; if they win, the world will be a more beautiful place in which to live. They have dedication and resolve, an inherent vision that will not accept defeat.

FREEDOM

*No one has a right to destroy
anything in the wilderness; such
things belong to all and must not
be disturbed. Freedom gives no
license to violate a heritage that
belongs to the ages.*

How often one hears the term "freedom of the wilderness" wondering what it really means. It is true, in a wilderness one does have certain freedoms to come and go at will, wind and weather permitting—freedom from the tyranny of time, and from having constantly to adjust—but there are limits imposed by nature on all creatures.

An overly aggressive beaver colony can eat itself out of house and home if it disregards the basic rules of population and survival. On one of my favorite trout streams—with a beautiful stretch of almost open meadow where one could use a fly freely without the constant hazard of getting caught in a treetop or tangle of brush, the bottom ideal for wading, with little riffles and logs, and dark holes under the banks—a beaver colony moved in to harvest all the aspen and birch within reach. That was the end of fly-fishing, and before long a dam was built across the lower end, backing up the water several feet, with a huge house midway upstream. It was impossible to wade because of the depth and deposition of black silt over the old hard bed of sand and gravel I had known. In a few years the aspen and birch were gone, but that did not deter the beaver, for then they started on the fringing border of alder and dwarf birch and willow, until the entire flat was practically denuded of vegetation. Their canals ran far into the woods and to step into one meant going down into a boggy hole often waist deep. Finally—and this took about ten years—there was no more food except on the distant hillside beyond the reach of the canals. Only then did the beaver leave.

The dam was soon broken by spring floods and the water returned to normal; the silt began to wash out and the bottom became clean and hard again. I made a trip to the stream just a year ago, and to my delight it looked as it used to. Willow, young alder, and scrub birch were coming back and I was happy to recognize old rocks behind which there were always trout. It did not take the stream long to recover its character, nor the trout to come in and find the places they had known for many years.

Moose can also eat themselves out of forage, as they did on Isle Royale before a pack of wolves moved in one winter on the ice. I can still see the balsams and cedars browsed almost down to the ground and moose rapidly dying of starvation. With a pack of wolves to keep them in check, the browse has come back and the pack has not increased, a classic example of population in balance.

On the Kaibab Plateau of Arizona, the deer, without the presence of predators, soon reached such proportions they were dying by hundreds and thousands before hunting was allowed. And so it is everywhere: the freedom of the wilderness demands its own controls or disaster results.

Modern man feels he is a creature who can disregard any controls of population or food. He violates the ancient taboos, the "Thou shalt nots," and thinks he can do pretty much as he wants, if he can get by with it. In pioneer days, he felt he had the right to kill and desecrate, destroying not only his environment but the right of other creatures to enjoy it. Now, with the frontier gone, we see the fallacies of our actions. We still presume we own the land, however, and think we can do with it as we wish, refusing to recognize that no one really owns it. Indians believe the land is God's and no one has the right to manipulate it, that it is to be used not only by man but equally by all living creatures. Since it belongs to God, man has not the right to buy, sell, or mistreat it in any way, or destroy it if he so wills.

Our young are in revolt against restrictions of any kind, but they do not realize unlimited freedom means chaos. This has always been, and always will be. There are some things that simply cannot be done. This is particularly true where numbers have grown out of control, as they have in our urban concentrations, and even in the wilderness regions set aside for their enjoyment. What they fail to see is that crowding anywhere in the wilderness means loss of freedom, and more regulation in order to maintain its character.

Many come to such a wilderness as the Boundary Waters Canoe Area of Minnesota and feel the bars are down, that they have the right to cut green trees for firewood, inundate campsites with their litter and debris, make the nights hideous with noise, and the days as well. Wilderness should be sacred and quiet, just as the Indians felt in designating certain places as spirit lands where no one talked. I have written about the Kawashaway River country of "no place between," where the Indians always traveled quietly and spoke only in whispers. To many young people who do not know, this dictum is violated by the sheer volume of their clamor, and so they deny themselves two of the greatest values of wilderness travel, solitude and silence.

What applies to silence applies as well to our treatment of others in the wilds. Long ago, when I was a guide and there was unlimited room, to see another canoe on the lake I had chosen to camp on was an affront, to run into other parties on a portage an equal annoyance. Today it is different, for portages are often crowded and there is always a race for popular campsites. But, even so, the old rules exist and should be observed as much as possible. No one should invade another's privacy if he can avoid it, and if there is room for several tents, each party should be aware of the others' enjoyment.

The matter of common courtesy is still alive and important. It is discourteous in the extreme to leave a campsite littered and without firewood. How pleasant to find one where the fire is laid with birch bark and a handful of dry sticks, with enough wood beside it to make a good fire should a new party come in after dusk. How great to have tent poles stacked safely against a tree. This sounds like a lack of freedom to do as we like, but it should be interpreted as the freedom to make others happy and therefore ourselves.

What applies to campsites applies equally to personal cleanliness. Of course you can look as messy as you choose, but the fact remains that in nature filth means disease and death. Animals keep themselves spotlessly clean and spend much time grooming their fur or feathers, not for personal vanity, but because it is a matter of health and survival.

There is also the impact psychologically of cleanliness. No excuse is good enough for not washing body and clothes, or for putting dishes, pots, and pans covered with the remains of food or soot from the fire into a food pack. I have met many wilderness travelers, not only in my home country but far in the North, and one look at some of them and their outfits tells me how they will react with respect to common courtesies and the country. They are the ones who leave campsites dirty, chop up tent poles rather than leave them for others, and after cleaning fish either leave the skins, heads, and entrails on the rocks or throw them into the water just off shore. They are the kind who leave beer cans and Coke bottles—or, worse, break them on the rocks—who mutilate Indian pictographs or portage signs, and use tables and benches for firewood. They give themselves away immediately, and seldom am I wrong in my estimate of their boorishness.

Freedom of the wilderness means many things to different people. If you really want to enjoy it, you must recognize your responsibilities as adult humans living in a world with others. No one has a right to kill chipmunks, squirrels, whisky jacks, seagulls, or any other form of life which adds interest to a wilderness campsite. They are a large part of the wilderness enjoyment, as much a part as lichens on the rocks, as trees, shrubs, and mosses, as the vistas of fleets of floating islands in the distance, as the roar of rapids. Such things belong to everyone and must not be disturbed. Freedom gives no one license to change a heritage that belongs to the ages.

TRADITION

*My two old canoes are works of art
embodying the feeling of all canoemen
for rivers and lakes and the wild country
they were built to traverse. They were made
in the old tradition when there was time
and love of the work itself.*

I have two canvas-covered canoes, both old and beauti-
fully made. They came from the Penobscot River in Maine
long ago, and I treasure them for the tradition of craftsmanship in their construction, a pride not only of form and line
but of everything that went into their building. When I look
at modern canoes, of metal or fiberglass stamped out like so
many identical coins, I cherish mine even more, knowing how
different canoe builders felt about their work when they were
made.

The older one is a Morse-Vezie, which came into this
country during the early exploration in the 1880's. Sixteen
feet in length, it has graceful lines with a tumble home or
curve from the gunwales inward, much the same as the early
ships built to carry ore from the mines of the Vermilion and
Mesabi Ranges down the Great Lakes. Whalebacks they
called them, and the ships actually looked like whales and

slipped as smoothly through the water. No canoe I've ever used paddles as easily as the Morse-Vezie, because of this feature. The gunwales and the decks are of mahogany, the ribs and planking of carefully selected spruce and cedar. My canoe, built by Morse from the little town of Vezie, was paddled on Burntside Lake in the early days, and was finally put into storage in a warehouse loft where I found it many years later.

The other canoe was built by the White brothers at Old Town, Maine, also on the Penobscot River. Slightly different in shape, it incorporates the finest features of their famous Guides' Model. In my correspondence with one of the White brothers—penciled notes on scraps of yellow paper—he insisted if I did not like the canoe, I could return it; they had put one of their best men to work on it and hoped I would be pleased. When it came, I was more than happy; it was exactly what I wanted, and I knew for them doing a good job was more important than the money involved. Tradition, care, and attention to the smallest detail went into it. This one, too, paddles like a dream, gives me the feeling it is more than a canoe, a work of art embodying the love of all canoemen for rivers and lakes and the wild country it was built to traverse.

It disturbs me to note the loss of the old traditions that came into being from the time men made things with their hands. Tools were important and pioneers often forged and tempered their own. There was more time to do work well, and craftsmanship was a matter of pride and, often, survival.

I look at my old cabin built by early settlers almost as long ago as my two canoes: hardly a line between the jackpine logs, the marks of the broadax still plain, the corners of the dog-neck type used in Finland, a bond that held the logs together with only an occasional wooden peg for strength.

The original owners must also have looked at it with pride. It was made to last, to keep out the winter's cold and the summer's storms. There was reason for the economy and skill and painstaking work that went into it.

I own an old Finnish knife or *puukko,* the blade made from an old file, the handle and molded case of birch bark. I have carried it for thousands of miles and it has never failed me. The well-tempered steel is hard enough to open a tin and still sharp enough to fillet a fish without needing retouching. Not long ago I dropped it while I was at Listening Point, and traced and retraced my steps without avail. A young friend, Al Cooper from Utah, was there, and we literally combed the area where we had walked. Since it was early November, the smell of snow was in the air, and we knew if we did not find it then, it would lie outdoors all winter.

"Let's go back once more," Al said before dusk settled down. "We just might be lucky."

Back we went, looking into the grasses and heather, under the spreading branches of pine and juniper, hoping against hope we might catch a glint of steel. Then, with a shout of triumph, my young friend ran over and placed the knife in my hand. Before he left, he took a picture of me standing by the cabin turning the knife over and over. Far more than a tool, the knife is to me a symbol of the spirit that went into the cabin, the canoes, and all things made by men proud of their work and of what they had learned to do.

There is a certain dignity that comes to those who use their hands in doing something well, a calm assurance at having conceived an object and seeing it through to its completion, which is missing in production lines where workers often do only one essential task and never see the finished product.

Hanging on the wall of my cabin is a pair of Indian

moccasins with exquisite beadwork and leather soft as silk given to me by a Cree Indian woman. She used no model for her design, and as I watched her work, I knew somewhere deep within her there was an infallible rule of measurement gauged only by a glance, an inborn sense of color and artistry, part of the legendry of her race. She was proud of what she had done, and I, too, was proud when she gave them to me. Those moccasins could have been made in a shoe factory, but they would not have had the personal touch, or the joy I saw in her eyes when she knew I was happy with her handiwork.

I think of the abandonment of the old Puritan work ethic and the current feeling among many that work is something to be avoided at all costs. People seem to have forgotten an important truth: that work is dignified, no matter what it may be, as long as it is of use personally, to the family, or to society. For a long time work took most of our days, leaving little leisure for other pursuits. It is also true much of the drudgery is now taken care of by machines and innumerable devices for lessening the labor once so taken for granted it was the goal of existence.

What we have lost in the process of mechanization is the simple fact there can be a joy in work that is found no other way. Labor, no matter what it is, can be its own reward. It does not have to be a work of art, or creative in the sense of involving mind and imagination, but if one looks at it as contributing to the general welfare, the most menial task can be worthwhile and add a certain dignity. No task need consume a mind entirely; one can think and dream even though the body is committed. There is also no reason a man doing dull physical work cannot, during his evenings or whenever he happens to be free, enjoy music, literature, or some artistic pursuit of his own; no reason work as an ethic should be the sum total of existence.

That is why natives everywhere are looked at askance for their apparent indolence by so-called civilized man imbued with constant industry toward the goal of material gain. Ask any native to explain the difference in attitude, and it is difficult for him. Life to the native does not mean eternal labor, but rather a world of spirit without tension, deadening drudgery, and ultimate physical and mental exhaustion. The revolt of many today against work is a reaction to the loss of identity man has suffered since the birth of the industrial age. We must never forget, however, the danger of losing pride in work if we abandon entirely what we now seem to condemn.

While I was in Alaska recently, I read a delightful book entitled *One Man's Wilderness,* recounting the adventures of Richard Proenneke as told to his friend Sam Keith. Proenneke had a lifetime dream of going into the Alaskan bush to build a cabin of his own without help from anyone. He chose a place in the foothills of the Alaska Range beyond Clark's Pass, a beautiful spot near a little lake with a great mountain range behind it. He picked up a few tools, selected his site carefully, and spent a year doing what he had always wanted to do. The felling of trees was a joy in itself; they were not so large he could not handle them alone, or drag them to the building site. He figured out exactly how he wanted his corners and how much space to allow between the logs. He treasured his tools, took good care of them; finally got the roof on, covering it with moss and grass, with the logs tightly chinked, and a fireplace built. When he was through, he looked at it with a pride and satisfaction he had never known before. It would have been much easier to have materials flown in, as were his food and other supplies, but the work itself counted most with him.

He did not indulge in philosophical explanations or in

any way try to justify his work, and I do not suppose it would have been possible for him to explain adequately how he felt, more than for any bushwacker or native, what it meant to accomplish a task for the sheer love of doing it. That is what this chapter is about, a plea to return if we can to a world of sanity in our attitude toward the tasks we have to do, an attempt to hold on to something meaningful. We can never revert entirely to the old days, but we must remember there are other satisfactions in work that can be enjoyed, together with those our affluence has showered us with, rewards possible now because of the new leisure time we have.

WHOLENESS

Wholeness is the sum total
of wilderness experience; it is the
ephemeral essence, the ultimate
that puts one in tune with cosmic values.

To explain wholeness, one must go back to the very depths of being, for it is involved with all that has gone before—man's entire evolution and the imprint of millennia on his consciousness. It is harmony and oneness, the very antithesis of fragmentation, emptiness, and frustration. It means being alive and aware of all about you and all that has ever been. It is being in tune with waters and rocks, with vistas and horizons, with constellations and the infinity of time and space.

When Henry Beston, who in *Outermost House* wrote the story of his life on Cape Cod, said "Wholeness is being in tune with the wind, sand, and stars," he spoke the truth, for that is exactly what it is, being in tune.

Even in the wilderness one must wait until all evidence of civilization is erased. I felt it not long ago while sitting at the end of a long glaciated spit of rock in the Quetico-Superior country. It was perfectly calm, the lake glassy and mirrored with the deeply colored sunset, loons calling as though possessed, and because it was spring the hermit thrushes were singing. I was alone with a sense of such completeness, I desired nothing more.

Wholeness is part of simplicity and silence, and of all the components of a wilderness experience. It creeps up without warning, cannot be sought or looked for, but suddenly it is there. One never says, "This is wholeness," for at the time he thinks of nothing and often does not realize he has known it until long afterward. But once having felt it, he never forgets. This is the essence, the ultimate.

Some years ago I met Father Moraud on the Churchill River in northern Manitoba. He had spent half a century in that country serving the Crees as far north as Cree Lake. Though a member of a distinguished French-Canadian family, he had chosen to spend his life in the wilds administering to his flock. He was the epitome of all men of the cloth who over the centuries of exploration had gone into the far reaches of the North giving their lives to spread the gospel of Christianity.

Once he came to visit me, refused to spend any time in town, and insisted on going to my cabin on Listening Point where he would feel more at home. I shall never forget the picture of him saying his prayers on a bare ledge just beyond the cabin, looking toward the west. He went out each evening alone after supper, and I can see his black silhouette kneeling there. If ever a man exuded a sense of wholeness, it was he. He knelt for a long time, part of the North he had become, of many expeditions by canoe, snowshoe, and dog team, of the bitter cold and near starvation, but also of the serenity that comes when one knows he has given all and asked for nothing. When he returned to the cabin, he brought with him the calm he had known, a sense of peace. We talked for a while before the fireplace and then he was ready for bed. It was always the same; it never varied and I did not disturb him. It would have been a sacrilege.

I have a picture of Father Moraud in my mind standing in the bow of his big freighter canoe, his cassock blowing in the wind, bowing from the waist as the courtier he was, then raising his hands in blessing as we swept by. Wholeness, serenity, and peace were in his face.

Serenity comes from wholeness, and one finds it in strange places. Once in a large city, while I was riding a subway, a woman took a seat just opposite mine. She was neither young nor old, but for some reason the profile of her face struck me, and it was not until she turned and smiled briefly that I saw the serenity in her eyes. I wanted to talk to her but did not dare, and though this happened many years ago, I have never forgotten the look on her countenance. She got off shortly and I watched her go with regret, but her serenity left itself with me. What gave her a sense of peace and wholeness I shall never know.

My feeling of wholeness seems to come while I am in the middle in the wilds, most often when I am alone, but also with someone who understands as I do. Paddling with Elizabeth when our strokes are timed as one, it comes often, or when we are sitting quietly on some high lovely place. We are a part of the silence together.

My sauna gives me a sense of wholeness, for after breathing in the fragrance of cedar, basking in the hot steam, then plunging into the lake, I experience inevitably a sense of relaxation and removal, complete, and utterly without distraction. After it is over, I often lie on the rough gray planks of my dock, listen to the chuckle of water beneath me, and watch the sunlight against the cedars, at peace with the world. I may not be serene in the true sense of the word, but there is a sense of wholeness.

The same feeling comes when, after fighting the waves for a long day with many hours of straining muscles to their utmost, you finally reach the hoped-for goal and see a shore that for hours had been a misty line in the horizon. It is almost miraculous to see its rocks and trees materialize with the promise of a shelter somewhere among them. After the swift labor of setting up a campsite, and with supper eaten and nothing more to do, there too is a sense of wholeness.

During the day, you are part of the waves, judging them, coasting down the long slopes between, only to climb to the top of another and then do it over again, until you are completely drained of energy. Somehow the mind is washed clean, and when it is over the cleanness continues until you crawl into your bag for hours of dreamless sleep.

A man can work just as strenuously in town, exhaust himself entirely, but in the process it is somewhat different, for the exhaustion is amplified by noise and clamor that take away the peace of rest. One eats, changes clothes, relaxes, but there is none of the utter forgetfulness I know in the wilds. We are all different and cannot tell what another feels, but the formula is infallible for me.

Wholeness is an ephemeral thing, combining all the wilderness epitomizes or at times only a few of its qualities, but however it may be, it puts one in tune with cosmic forces and makes him part of timelessness and mystery. As Bertrand Russell once said: "It is possible to live in so large a world the vexations of daily life come to feel trivial and the purposes which stir our deeper emotions take on something of the immensity of our cosmic contemplations. If mankind can acquire this kind of wisdom, our new powers over nature offer a prospect of happiness and well-being such as men have never experienced before."

PART THREE

The Imponderables

*The divine spark is within us all,
and when we are conscious of it, we touch
the eternal and the great truths that
have come from the minds and hearts
of men.*

THE INTANGIBLES

*You can measure soil, water,
and trees, but intangibles never.*

There are intangible values in works of art that have always been taken for granted. Not long ago in one of our museums, I saw a woman standing engrossed before a great painting, her head bowed in reverence, and in her eyes a strange and happy light. What she saw in that painting certainly was not the canvas, its beautiful frame, or the amount of oil and pigment the artist had used, but something intangible which inspired her as it had thousands of others. If asked, she would find it difficult to explain, but one could see it affected her deeply.

Is it ever possible to explain the intangible values of a Beethoven sonata or a great poem—Gray's "Elegy," perhaps, or Bryant's "To a Waterfowl"? What do the following lines mean to you?

Whither midst falling dew,
While glow the heavens with the last steps of day . . .

If you happen to be a duck hunter, you know they are far more than words. They embody sunsets on the marshes, the whisper of wings at dawn, things others do not know. Bryant caught it in two lines, the intangibles of ducks against the sky.

Intangible values are hard to define, explain, or measure. You can measure soil, water, and trees, but intangibles never. Even so let us try, if we can, to gain some idea of what they are and how they fit into the environmental picture. We do know they stir the emotions, influence happiness, and thereby make life worth living. They are involved with the good life, but sometimes I wonder if we know what the good life really is. They are so important that without them it loses its meaning.

We talk about the intangible values of environmental protection and know we cannot embark on any effort or program of conservation without them. Back of all concrete problems, the intangibles are the ultimate key. They give substance to the practical, provide reasons for everything we do, and are so involved and integrated with conservation efforts it is impossible to separate them.

There is no question about the intangible values I have experienced in the outdoors, and I am convinced that in conservation and all the efforts toward preserving the environment, they play an enormous and powerful role. There have been many definitions of conservation. Aldo Leopold said, "It is the development of an ecological conscience." It would take a long time to explain exactly what he meant, but I believe he implied unless we develop a feeling for the land and an understanding of it, unless we become one with it and recognize love, stewardship, and above all an appreciation of its intangible values, we cannot fully comprehend what conservation means.

Louis Bromfield stated, "Conservation is living in harmony with the land"; Joseph Wood Krutch, "Conservation without love of the land is meaningless"; and Paul Sears, of

Yale, "Conservation is a point of view involved with the whole concept of freedom, dignity, and the American spirit." In other words, conservation is a basic philosophy and a way of life.

What do we mean by a way of life? If we judge it by our affluence and the fact that we have more of the amenities and luxuries than any other people on earth, then to many it means exactly that. When we consider the short span of our occupancy of this virgin continent and realize what we have done to it, I doubt if we have any right thinking we have had a good life. What we have enjoyed during our pioneer period we have taken for granted as our due, and during the past few decades we have lived a life of luxurious abandonment of environmental responsibility. I doubt if we have any understanding of the true meaning of an ecological conscience.

Most Americans will agree the good life has been one of plenty, of breathing space, freedom, and an outdoors of indescribable variety and beauty; it meant the opportunity of carving out our destinies before the days of the frontier were ended. Now with more of our people living in urban concentrations and the great open spaces succumbing to the agribusiness concept of farming, with less and less contact with the land itself, we begin to wonder. Are we heading toward a mechanized civilization where the good life, as we have thought of it, is going to disappear? Are we going to continue mistreating our land to the point where the old American dream we had is gone forever?

Not long ago I flew over New York City. For some reason the great plane circled and circled over miles of tenements and slums, and as I looked down and pondered about the good life and the children who have never seen grass, trees, or clean running water, I wondered what their answer would be to the question of what the good life is.

I saw Central Park that day, a tiny green oasis far below, surrounded by the roaring bustling city. That natural area is worth uncounted billions, but I knew its intangible values to the people were far more important than any monetary consideration. There was a sanctuary of the spirit in the midst of one of the greatest industrialized cities of the world, a place beyond any normal concept of value, and I thought of an editor of the New York *Times* who, in writing about the program of preserving the Quetico-Superior area from the ravages of airplane development, said "Tranquillity is beyond price."

More and more we think of the relationship of natural resources to our way of living, our freedom to come and go and do the things we used to do. Sterling North summed it up when he said, "Every time you see a dust cloud, a muddy stream, a field scarred by erosions, or a channel choked with silt, you are witnessing the passing of American democracy."

One of our great historians, in telling of the migration of races from Asia toward the West, spoke of all that remains —only dust and mounds of rubble marking the palaces, pyramids, and temples that once sparkled along those ancient lanes of travel. Archeologists have unearthed ancient civilizations marking the glories of the past, glories that faded when people became decadent due to their affluence. What happened to them and why did they move and die? They died because they mistreated their land, their forests, and waters, failing until too late to recognize the intangible values of their homeland environments.

It is easier for me to think of the intangibles with respect to water than with most other resources, for I have always lived close to it. When I think of water, instinctively I think of the Quetico-Superior along the international border with Canada. Is the importance of that country its timber, vast deposits of iron and copper nickel, or its other material sources of wealth and continued affluence? There is no question of their role in our economy, but when I look out upon the lake from my cabin, I know its real value lies in the realm of the intangibles, vistas of wilderness waterways, solitude, and quiet. Those, I am convinced, are the true values that someday in the future may far outshadow all others in importance. It is hard to put a price tag on such things, on sounds, smells, and memories you have loved, on the extra dividends of the good life.

Some years ago I was in the sequoias and remember how I felt, realizing those great trees were mature long before the continent was discovered and that their growth reached back to the very beginnings of Western civilization. I understood then how John Muir felt in his battle to preserve them, that they belonged to the solitudes and the millennia, not to grasping modern man.

Last summer The Nature Conservancy bought two islands in a quiet bay not far from my cabin. One of them has a stand of virgin timber with great red and white pines, some well over two hundred years of age. I used to paddle over to the island and rest beneath those trees where it was always still, the only sounds the twittering of kinglets and nuthatches high up in the sunlit tops. A pileated woodpecker also lived there and its tattoo on one of the old dead stubs sounded constantly. On the ground was a deep bed of pine needles out of which grew Linnaea, dwarf dogwood, and gold thread. It is a hallowed spot and I am glad it will be preserved for all time.

We need trees. We need them for industry and building and paper, and must have them for our particular way of life because they play a vital part in our economy, but we must never forget there is something in trees besides the practical.

Trees can be harvested, but should never be cut where they stand in places of beauty, with outstanding intangible values so evident there can be no question. That island is one of them.

A constant effort is necessary to save such areas from exploitation. With growing population and people more and more removed from close contact with the earth and those values which for ages have molded us, there is great need for men to come in touch with silence, cyclic rhythms, and natural beauty if they are to retain their perspective. Tension, speed, and lack of real purpose in their daily lives make it mandatory they go to places where they can find themselves, regain their dignity and fulfillment as humans.

It is the intangible values of the land they need. The conservation of waters, forests, mountains, and wildlife are far more than saving terrain. It is the conservation of the human spirit which is the goal, and that is what is meant by the good life, one with the opportunity to find peace and quiet somewhere beyond where they happen to live. The last year of record indicates there were over two hundred million visitors to national parks, monuments and historical areas, wildlife refuges, the wilderness regions of national forests, state and federal preserves, proof in itself of the growing urgency. It is encouraging to know programs setting aside more areas are meeting with overwhelming public support. Perhaps we are emerging from the attitudes of the frontier. If this is true, and I believe it is deep-rooted in our national consciousness, then there is hope for America and the world.

LOVE OF
THE LAND

*Love of the land is the basis
for the unending struggle of those
who really care against those
who see only material rewards.*

Without love of the land, conservation lacks meaning or purpose, for only in a deep and inherent feeling for the land can there be dedication in preserving it. Love has many meanings, and it is harder to speak of with respect to environment than of one's attachment to another person. However it is interpreted, love is the lodestone that makes possible the sacrifice of time, energy, and money required to carry on any effort to save a portion of the natural scene or the earth itself from the impact of man's manipulations.

Love involves sensitivity, a sense of stewardship and concern. One can love a flower for its beauty, a rock for its permanence and stability, or a tree for its meaning in the kaleidoscope of vegetational change. One can love an animal and cherish the return of its affection; love has to do with associations over the years, some particular place where a person has known happiness with others.

One can be enchanted by a vista for the same reason, or by a way of life. Love, as someone said, "is a many-splendored thing" involving the whole broad realm of human experience. What is love but deep emotional reaction welling up from the depths of being? It is embedded in our subconscious, no doubt had its birth when some sensitive individual placed a flower on the burial place of a departed friend or left a bit of food for the long journey into the unknown, or possibly stood in mute reverence and shock, with a sense of loss and bereavement. From such early intimations grew the concept of tolerance and attachment and personal involvement that today we encompass broadly in the simple word "love."

It is part of a maturing spiritual response, and we see natives today in many parts of the world leaving things of value on a burial place. During my early years, it was not uncommon to find such offerings on the grave of an Indian— some trinket the departed one had treasured. I recall one particularly in the Far North where a paddle had been left; the grave was grown over with tundra and mosses and the little enclosure had fallen down, but the paddle was there, a worn blade bleached and whitened by the snows of many winters and the rains of summers. One who knows the significance of a paddle on the waterways knows what it meant. On another, in the Quetico-Superior, was an ancient little phonograph, one of the first, and I thought of the happy times it had provided at feasts and gatherings of the past when its music lightened the hearts of family and friends. I remember little houses built over shallow graves, each with a small hole in the end for the spirit to come and go. I stopped often at such places, where Indian companions left a little food or tobacco, just for old time's sake.

I think of the pyramids of ancient Egypt erected at the cost of countless lives to house the remains of departed kings. Arrogance, perhaps—pride and a belief in personal divinity were no doubt the reasons for the tremendous structures, but even back of that must have been the original primeval feeling for those who had gone.

We often hear people say they love a place, a flower, an individual, and we must not scoff, for it is emotion in its purest sense and one must not be ashamed of showing or expressing it. Life without deep feeling is a barren waste, sterile, cold, and meaningless.

I have read of the monk in *The Brothers Karamazov* who on his deathbed told his followers, "Love all the earth, every ray of God's light, every grain of sand or blade of grass, every living thing. If you love the earth enough, you will know the divine mystery."

Love is not sentimental or frivolous. It is a true feeling with many connotations, the motive power for all we do to preserve the land or a way of life we feel is good. Love of beauty, awareness, and understanding of the issues involved form the basis for the unending struggle of those who really care against those who see in the land only a source of material reward.

In a lifetime of trying to preserve wilderness, I have seen love's impact and known its power. Those who oppose destruction or unwise exploitation are accused of being sentimental and impractical. Standing forests have been called "cellulose cemeteries" by those who would destroy them; the fighters have been dubbed the "daffodil fringe of conservation." After a hike along the coast of Olympic National Park to demonstrate the tragedy of building a highway down its length, we were met with an enormous banner across the end of the trail near the little Indian village of La Push: "BIRD WATCHERS GO HOME." We had spent five glorious days along that coast, watched the waves breaking against the pinnacled stacks out from shore, studied the tidal pools with their color and myriad forms of life, climbed the cliffs of points being cut off by the incoming tides from the open sea, had seen what a highway from Lake Ozette in the north would do to this last magnificent stretch of shore. "BIRD WATCHERS GO HOME." As I looked at that banner, I thought how little the opposition really knew of what the good life entailed, and what the shore of magnificent rocks and the rolling Pacific surf really meant. The fact that we won our battle is proof of the power of love, the dedication that went with it, and its growing influence in the world, especially in the young of America who have caught the vision since Earth Day a few years ago.

Countless groups have been spawned in coalitions of various kinds to carry on the never-ending struggle. The Minnesota Public Interest Research Group (MPIRG) is a good example, with over ninety thousand members from a dozen or more colleges and universities in the state, financed by a deduction of one dollar from each student and supported by the institutions involved. The members of the Minnesota group have involved themselves with practically every environmental problem in the state, but what is important is their growing political sophistication—the need for working with the state legislature, agencies of federal government, zoning boards of counties, townships, and municipalities— their realization that only in this way can they achieve their goal. Their interests cover everything from wilderness preservation of the Boundary Waters Canoe Area to the impact of taconite and copper-nickel mining and setting aside small preserves everywhere. MPIRG is typical of citizens' groups all over the country who are becoming more and more effective.

I think back to my own early experience in the Quetico-Superior country, when our first battles were fought by a handful of men who, because of their feeling for the canoe country, dedicated themselves to its preservation. They did not fight because of any interest in the material values of the area's resources, but for their love of something they had found beyond price.

It is interesting to remember these battles are won because of the deep convictions of those who want to save parts of beautiful America, a desire based on feeling and devotion. While they may know failure and delay, they never forget. Exploiters whose desires are based only on the material do forget, and it is this factor that often means victory.

An old prospector friend of mine, who has been looking for the mother lode most of his life, told me it was not the gold that counted, but the eternal search, the sound of some creek he was working on, the quiet and peace, the feeling of being alone in the wilds. To take him from all this and transport him to the cities would have meant death. Love of what he was doing, with all its rewards, was what counted.

There are many broadly and nationally based citizens' groups such as the Wilderness Society, the Sierra Club, the Izaak Walton League, the Audubon Society, the Nature Conservancy, the National Parks Association, and the Wildlife Federation, with total memberships of several million. These are very effective, because they reach into every corner of the land and their members know how government works and what must be done.

In Canada citizens' groups are also burgeoning and it is encouraging to see how they, too, have learned the lesson— that to save the land is to become politically involved. I met with the Canadians not long ago and found the same deep sense of dedication, which inspires action and accomplishment. They also have broadly based national groups and coalitions, such as the Federation of Nature and the Conservation Council of Ontario, composed of scientists, government, and university people, as well as the Algonquin Wildlands League and the Quetico Foundation. No longer are those concerned about the land lone voices in the wilderness. At last they are being heard and listened to with respect and understanding.

FLASHES
OF INSIGHT

*Flashes of insight or reality
are sunbursts of the mind.*

There are certain moments when one sees more clearly, the world stands out more distinctly, and one's vision is unclouded and crystalline. Such instances are rare and come usually without warning, but they are worth waiting for and must be savored to the full. In my book *The Singing Wilderness*, I describe one of them:

> I once climbed a great ridge called Robinson Peak to see the sunset and a view of the lakes and rivers below, the rugged hills and valleys of the Quetico-Superior. When I reached the bald knob of the peak, the sun was just above the horizon, a flaming ball ready to drop into the dusk. Far beneath me on a point of pines reaching into the lake was the white inverted V of my tent. It looked very tiny down there where it was almost night.
>
> As I watched I became conscious of the slow steady hum of millions of insects and through it the last calling of the whitethroats and the violin notes of the hermit thrushes. It was very vague and far away

from that height and gradually merged one into the other, blending in a great all-enveloping softness of melody no louder than my breathing. The sun was trembling now on the edge of the ridge. It was alive, almost fluid and pulsating, and as it sank it seemed I could feel the earth turning it and actually feel its rotation. Here was that sense of oneness which comes when we listen with inward ears and see with inward eyes, when we are aware with our entire beings rather than our senses.

Life is a constant search for such moments, as it is for the singing or the elusive notes of the Pipes of Pan, and it is not surprising that they are often part of this experience, for one seldom becomes aware of any flash of reality without hearing the inner music.

Snatches of high insight, glimpses of beauty, stirrings of passion, excitement, or enthusiasm, communion with God may come when we are in harmony with the whole, at any time—in the eyes of a loved one, or the touch of a hand. One does not have to climb a Robinson Peak; it can be felt when looking at a blossom, smelling fresh rain, leaves, and needles, or sensing gladness in a child. The important thing is to be aware—never a day without some event that springs of the spirit.

This does not mean one must walk around with a childish view of things and events, but only be alive and recognize the moments when they happen. It need not be more than an instant; even that is enough. Daily glimpses of tenderness and swift understanding—a quickening of normal rhythms is what to watch for. Communion comes when experiences are in relationship to the driving forces of body and mind and union with the earth.

The divine spark is within us all, and when we use it in any way, we touch the eternal. Goethe counted any day lost in which he did not find some moment of beauty or spirit, some flash of absolute truth or goodness when he was conscious of a single all-encompassing unity.

Once on an early spring trip, when the snow was disappearing from the hillsides, the deer were migrating to the thawed places for food, and the snow on the ice of lakes had hardened into a firm crust, I sat in front of my log cabin facing a bay in the east. My companions had gone to fish for trout and would not return for several hours. I looked down the lake in the direction they had gone and lost sight of them as they passed through a narrows. For some reason I did not return to the cabin at once: the old silence was there, the sense of aloneness and oneness. A word would have spoiled it, but in that special moment the wilderness about me seemed unutterably clear and close, beautiful and serene. The moment was short-lived but enough to know here again was a flash of reality. I had stayed behind to cut some firewood, clean the cabin, and find fresh balsam boughs for the bunks. The chores had new significance now, the boughs were more resinous and fragrant, the chopping was a labor of love.

I sometimes think it comes as the Ross Light does, those last level rays of the sun which transform everything with new meaning and color, transfixing all it touches.

Once, at dusk, I skied down the Lucky Boy Trail and stopped to rest at the end of Jack Pine Point overlooking a meadow where deer often crossed. A strong wind was blowing and the dry snow swirled above the clearing. As I leaned on my poles, a doe leaped through the meadow as though pursued by wolves, but none came into sight and the deer disappeared into the shadows. Before me was all the wildness I had known. This was what I had been searching for all my many years. The world stood out more closely then, and my vision unclouded for just a moment as my skis hissed across the meadow. I moved without effort in an aura of snow and light.

My son told of an experience he had while in Alaska that was similar to mine. He is a great skier, a former member of the ski troops of the 10th Mountain Division, and, knowing the trails he used, I could appreciate what he felt and saw. He told me of coming out of a spruce-grown muskeg into an open space on a moonlit night, when a movement in the open caught his attention—a moose, perhaps, or a wolf. As he watched, he saw it was a white-clad skier moving across the field, a ghostly wraith out of the past: ski troops in white parkas; his own days on patrol; the Finns in their desperate winter war against the Russians; the Norwegians on nightly commando raids against the Germans, swooping down upon them across the snow, making their strike in a blast of gunfire, and away as swiftly and silently as they had come. This lone figure epitomized those years of warfare in the snows, and in that moment it all came back to him with the same burning intensity I had known when a deer crossed my open space, crystallizing into a swift vision my wilderness experience.

What, one might ask, is reality? It is seeing the whole, complete without interference. Great artists, writers, creative people all over the world have sought for it—those moments when for some strange reason they see things they have never seen before, colored perhaps not only by their constant search but by an insight which comes from the subconscious. Sunbursts of the mind: it is the impact that counts, the sense of the unusual and revealed hidden meaning.

The other morning my red pines were full of crossbills, the males in their gorgeous red and black. Though I had seen them many times, once, when the Ross Light hit them feeding on the bronze cones in the top of a tall spruce, was such a moment of clarity. This time I stood close, watching the way they used their strange parrotlike beaks, taking seeds out of the half-open cones. It was as though I had never really seen them before, nor been so conscious of their beauty—the deep red bordered with dark sable, the single streak of white along the wings—the fact that for once they were unafraid.

Many times after camp is made and chores are finished, there is a moment of quiet when reality comes and the outside world seems like a mirage. With a wilderness vista before me, the world's conflicts and confusions suddenly are unimportant, and I know within myself evil will pass, and the real world, the one of the spirit, will survive.

Not long ago at an old campsite, my mind was filled with things I had seen and read in my travels, and while I was immersed with my thoughts, the moment came again, a moment when violence, greed, and uncertainty were like the froth of foam that drifts down from rapids and piles up along the shores during a storm.

BALANCE
AND ORDER

*Nature is always in equilibrium,
and only when we manipulate it for
our own purposes do we contribute
toward imbalance.*

In an age of technology, with knowledge of the balance
and order that exist not only in the universe but in the most
minute molecular structure of the elements and living cells—
the power which controls everything, including the exquisite
interdependencies of all forms of life—one cannot help being
aware of the supreme logic that controls our lives.

The term "cosmic rhythms" has become almost a cliché.
We are so familiar with wisdom and all-encompassing ram-
ifications which dominate not only what we choose to call the
inanimate but the animate as well that the more we discover
the surer we are the line between them is very thin indeed and
may not be there at all.

Technology has produced chaos, say many of our savants,
and looking at the present state of the world, one must agree
this is not far from truth. With the end of resources and
energy in sight, without which our industrial world will come
to a halt, with the threat of an exploding world population
that cannot be fed, and the growing realization that industrial

growth may not be the answer, there seems no easy way out of our pyramiding difficulties.

Talk of zero growth is anathema to most, even though we know without a balanced world economy and wiser use of natural resources our civilization may well perish. As man contemplates the order of the universe and nature in all its manifestations, he is conscious of an enormous incongruity in the surge toward more and more, rather than trying to live with less and less. What system we see in nature, substantiated by our vast and growing understanding, is no longer an empty or nebulous thought we can ignore. Compared to this very obvious truth, our own imbalance is a major threat.

Many of the wise, centuries ago, pondered the meaning of this relationship as they watched the skies at night, marveled at eclipses of the sun and moon, the miracle of shooting stars speeding through the black void of space, but their observations had little practical value in solving problems of their time. We, too, ponder the heavens, knowing the comet of last year will return again and those who saw Halley's Comet just after the turn of the century may see it another time before they die. The stars of the Milky Way will be in the skies long after man is gone, as they were billions of years before he came.

If balance is part of the natural world, what is there in such knowledge that can be of value to modern man? As I survey the wilderness about me, its woods, waters, and living things, I know how fortunate I am to see a small portion of what is relatively untouched and unchanged; I know there can be no peace or any future for man without the same sort of balance in our lives, no ecological progression or evolutionary change. Nature is always in a state of equilibrium, and only when we manipulate it for our own purposes do we contribute toward imbalance. This could be the key to our problems. In our engrossment with material things, we do not fear or listen to the idea of inexhaustibility, but continue to pursue the goal of more affluence.

A basic ecological truth which we still ignore, is the interdependence and interaction of all living things, including man. This is the guiding principle underlying human destiny, and we know unless we choose wisely in the few decades ahead, the fragile and intricate web of life could become a web of death.

Aware at last of our relentless drive for economic development and an ever-higher standard of living at the expense of dwindling resources, and the swiftly mounting degradation of environment and beauty of the natural scene, we are beginning to realize our future course can no longer be at the expense of quality in our lives. Only when we see ourselves as members of a balanced community can we live successfully.

While we recognize our world responsibilities, our guiding philosophy should be the enhancement of life through a vast dissemination of environmental and social knowledge and the encouragement of practices that will protect and preserve the kind of world we want.

Lewis Mumford speaks of balanced men of the past— Thoreau, Whitman, Melville, and Jefferson—believing their pioneer surroundings preserved the very qualities they represented. I think back to Sophocles and Plato, to Aristotle and Marcus Aurelius, towering figures all, leaving us with the hope that even though our civilization may be crumbling and our fate sealed by our denial of human values and high purposes, there is still a chance.

Mumford concludes, "Against the domination of the machine we shall restore fresh energy to the word and the dream, bring forth ideal projects, plans and dramas to the whole personality and the community that sustains us. Whereas the machine has meant dehumanization, the new age will give primacy to the person, so ethics and humane arts will dominate. Our present task is to take to ourselves the order, balance and continuity we find in nature."

Harrison Brown, in *The Challenge of Man's Future*, speaks the same language. "The machine," he says, "has divorced man from the world of nature to which he belongs and in the process he has lost in large measure the powers of contemplation with which he was endowed. A prerequisite for the preservation of the canons of humanism is a re-establishment of our organic roots with our natural environment, and related to it the evolution of ways of life which encourage contemplation and the search for truth and knowledge. . . . To be sure, such things have no practical value and are seemingly unrelated to man's pressing need for food and living space, but they are as necessary to the preservation of humanism as food is necessary to the preservation of human life."

I, too, dream of a world where man's great creativity is blended with that of nature. The unknown values are those which will prove to be our critical resources, not metals or energy, but values within the mind and spirit of man himself, the human resources. To what extent can we subjugate our selfishness to generosity, ignorance to wisdom, hate to love?

In previous times during periods of crisis, it was only individual nations and certain cultures that were threatened. Today the destiny of all humanity is at stake.

Joseph Wood Krutch, fully aware of such sobering thoughts, says, "The answers are what will determine the character of our civilization. Ultimately the solution must be found in either a law of God or Nature."

"The world," he says, "continues to grow richer and more

powerful, but is now restless and apprehensive within. It has given way to an age of anxiety. The richest and most powerful civilization is also the most frightened. If we should become convinced man has a human nature and the greatest of his needs to create a condition suited to it, then a really new world might come into being. . . . Our salvation would mean getting rid of our love of the machine for its own sake, of our delight in small gadgets as well as the great. If we did, we might begin to recover from our hypnosis.

"Someday, we may again discover the humanities are something more than ornaments and graces, man's consciousness more interesting than the mechanically determined aspects of his behavior, and we may again be more concerned with what man is than what he has and what he can do. We might again take more pride in his intellect than his tools, take more pride in man the thinker than man the maker. We might come to realize the proper study of man is man."

One can read and study the books of many men, believe the conclusions of *The Club of Rome,* that we are in real trouble and can come out of it only by living more simply, with more consideration for the quality of life we know inherently is our most basic need. Balance in our use of the earth is the answer, and in the distribution of its riches, recognizing nations can no longer feel isolated or secure, nor ignore the needs of others less fortunate. If this means the integration of mankind with nature in its various forms, it also means the integration of all people on this earth. It is a planetary matter, not a local or national one.

The solution seems simple, but solving it is difficult because most do not comprehend what the ultimate penalty may be. All great minds—those of today, of ages past, and before technology was ever dreamed of—have come to the same conclusion. Chardin says, "The great thing for man is to have finally become able to know that he is man and to know that he knows. This no other creature can do. . . . Mind and spirit is as definite a power as nuclear energy, it is the force which eventually will control the universe."

KNOW THYSELF

*The ancient saying "know thyself"
is one of the most tantalizing admonitions
ever given to man.*

The ancient saying "know thyself," spoken by an oracle
of the temple of Apollo at Delphi, is one of the most tantalizing admonitions ever given to man. Philosophers have
pondered its meaning and scholars have written learned tomes
of their deductions about it. Christianity is steeped in it and
St. Paul makes much of it in his various epistles. The world
religions have worked it into their basic beliefs. It has become
an eternal challenge, but to modern man it is so involved
with dogma, psychic complexity, and ritual, the true significance is often lost.

It would be better if we did not stress its details, for in
our penchant for infinite ramification we have almost forgotten what we are trying to prove. Would it not be more pro-
ductive simply to look about and see in nature the mirror of
ourselves? We must recognize our interdependency, remembering knowledge and science, with their endless possibilities
of contradiction, can destroy understanding of a dictum so
profound as this.

One of the first steps in the direction of understanding is

to decide what kind of person you are by asking a few questions and answering them truthfully. As a naturalist, I speak only from that point of view, and to those with whom I am closely allied I shall make no scholarly approaches, attempt to reach no vague metaphysical conclusions, but stay strictly within the realm I know in my own personal experience.

As an example, I ask what motivates my life. What is the most important element in it? What brings the most enduring happiness? I know myself from this angle, and the answers are inordinately simple, for I am convinced that nature, in all its aspects and my relationship to it, is and always has been my guiding light.

It is more difficult for the young to know this much about themselves, and I remember when I was not quite sure which way I was going. One day while roaming the woods of the country north of the great Mesabi—or Giant's Range, as the Indians called it—these thoughts occurred to me: What if this life I am leading is not the right one? Could I live anywhere else and know the same joy? Will it last forever, or might I change and embrace a different environment? I shall never forget the shock those questions posed, the almost frightening realization that I truly did not know if I were on the right trail.

I did not get the answers that day, nor for some years afterward, but continued living the way I had, hoping the final decision would come. During part of this time I was unhappy and unsure, and nothing is more unsettling to a young person. Eventually the decision did come, for the more I learned and the more country I saw, the more secure I was in my original feeling that I must live in the wilderness, that there could be no shortcomings or deviations in following my goal to the end. There was no vision, no burning bush or a thundering pronouncement from on high, merely a knowing in my consciousness that the questions had been answered as I hoped they might. With that simple realization I was filled with an inner glow of happiness and content which has *never* left me.

I knew the real task was to bolster my belief through study and reading, and discovered to my delight that for two thousand years or more men pondering this question had come up with the same conclusions. Nature, I found, did not necessarily mean to others what it meant to me. To some it was the evolution of mind and recognition of the creative forces in the realms of thought and art, beauty, and religion—all a way of attaining fullness and contributing to man's cultural or humanitarian needs. If one wants to write, build, paint, or philosophize, he must do it, and accept it as a basic part of knowing himself.

The other night a young man came to see me about taking a rather hazardous canoe trip into the Far North. He wanted to follow one of the routes I had taken, but kept wondering if he should. He was apprehensive, somewhat unsure of his ability to negotiate the rapids and find his way, and in his eyes was a disturbed look. "Sir," he said, "what do you actually think?"

"If you really want to do it," I said, "if it means that much to you, there is no choice but to go ahead."

"I want to be positive," he replied, "and something deep inside tells me I must."

I told him if that were the way he really felt and did not accept the risk, he would regret it the rest of his life. "You cannot turn your back on any challenge, physical or mental. If you do, you diminish yourself, and the next time it will be easier to say, 'No, I cannot do it.' If you take the hazards as they come and survive, you will be stronger and better and the trip will be a milestone in your life, one you will always know as a turning point."

This seemed to satisfy him, for I caught a new glint of joy and determination in his troubled eyes. I knew from long experience with many young men his age he would come through with colors flying and find out more about himself than he had ever known.

An old friend, who has lived most of his life in cities but had spent some time in the bush, wrote me recently. "The closer I come to the end," he confided, "the more important it is to know the wind is still blowing through those pines at your cabin. As long as I remember, I am comforted, for this is what I know best about myself. I have lived in many places, done many things, seen much of the world, but that sound in the trees seems all I have ever really wanted. It will give me peace until the day I die."

When I think of the many who do not know who they are, I remember the line from the famous Broadway play *The Man in the Grey Flannel Suit,* when the son, standing at the bier of his father, says to himself, "Poor guy, he never knew who he was." It is the only line I recall, but in it was a great truth, for many go through life not knowing themselves or who they really are.

Thoreau said, "I would not want to die knowing I had not lived." He knew himself as few men did, so well in fact there was no question about who he was or what he stood for. It reverberates in everything he wrote—no doubt of his having lived to the fullest.

There are many without the courage to shape their careers, intimidated by obvious dangers, secure only in the thought of a future that might provide the necessities of food and shelter, a good pension plan with no worry about retirement. I think of the many young Americans who have lost the courage to accept challenges of a more precarious existence, with riches of the spirit to replace guaranteed comfort and affluence. The young man who wondered about taking the canoe trip made the right decision, and I knew he would come away from his experience with moral strength and spiritual rejuvenation that he had never dreamed he possessed. True, the frontier days are past, but there are others just as challenging: frontiers of the mind and a drastic change in life-style to more simplicity, with rewards other than material.

I have great faith in the youth of America, for more and more are coming to this conclusion, knowing within themselves it is the right course to follow. The big answer was shaped by a decade of violence, confrontation, inflation, and unrest, with the prospect of world starvation and a degrading environment, the threat of nuclear conflict and the specter of survival itself looming constantly over the horizons. These youths have been tempered by what they have seen and known, and are willing to give of themselves in any way they can to make this a better and happier world to live in. This they seem to be absolutely sure of. They know there is much to learn, but also that action begins with each individual, and if he can act as a leavening in the dream of the future, life will be full and rich. If they continue and do not lose their ideals, each will know it is worthwhile and never need face his end with any wondering.

I think of the admonition "know thyself" with greater respect and simplicity than ever before, and am confident most who read what I have written will accept and understand my reactions. No two people will ever have the identical approach to the old saying, neither will its message deteriorate in value as a guideline to all mankind.

CONTEMPLATION

*Unplanned contemplation comes
softly as falling mist,
or the first snows of autumn.*

There has been much written during the past decade about
the joys of contemplation or meditation, of learning to com-
mune with one's inner self, stressing the detachment or divorcement of self from all disturbing influences. Yoga has
become a byword, each group with its own guru, prophet, or
leader, who must be followed blindly on the road to unspeak-
able happiness and content. Countless groups have prolifer-
ated all over the world until it seems there must be a great
hunger among those who have embraced the new cults, a
search going on desperately for something to hold on to which
will give meaning to their lives.

We hear about setting the stage, assuming the lotus posi-
tion, of attaining complete relaxation and removal, both
physically and mentally, in order to achieve the hoped-for
result of communion with God. I do not decry or belittle in
the slightest those ancient men of wisdom and light, or the
faiths that have become a way of life for millions in the
eternal quest for truth and wisdom.

But for one who has spent much time in the wilds, there

are simpler ways to arrive at the same result. Great minds have wrestled with the problems of humanity through many different ways of contemplation, from which has come advice of value and comfort to confused and puzzled modern man, but I do feel there is much to be said for simplicity devoid of the complexities of sects, creeds, and formulas.

Life in the wilderness, especially when one is alone, is a continual contemplation and communion with God and Spirit regarding eternal values. One does not have to assume any particular stance, invoke incantations, repeat over and over again words such as "Oom," chant, or sing. To me these are merely hypnotic devices used to bring the mind into focus and into the realm of silence by those who do not have the privilege of living in situations where peace is all about them. There is no doubt of the efficacy of such ways of preparation or they would not be followed by hundreds of thousands, but when quiet is all around, with no sounds but natural ones —bird songs, wind, washing of waters against the shores— the stage is always set for meditation and reflection, whatever one may choose to call it. Man may not be conscious of contemplation or seeking wisdom, for often no revelations come. Normal and unplanned contemplation comes as softly as the falling rain or the first snows in late fall when the entire world is waiting. While no great answers may come at these times, they do infiltrate occasionally and unobtrusively into one's consciousness, but usually there is simply a sense of peace, removal, and a happiness beyond understanding.

As I look back, I know there are certain experiences which invariably bring this sense of communion; quiet is not always the key, or concentrating on some pinpoint over the horizon, which erases thoughts, ideas, or problems from one's mind.

There is joy in finding new campsites, a place no one has camped before, where the rocks have not been moved since they were dropped by the great glacier ten thousand years before, rocks unscuffed by human feet and covered with lichens and mosses of many hues. In such a haven there are no scars or ax marks, no indications of use by others. To me they are holy and sacred and must not be disturbed, and I am careful to step softly around patches of caribou moss so as not to crunch the brittle growth with a careless step, for one has the feeling there of being part of the primeval.

Dr. Lin Yutang says in *The Wisdom of India and China:* "If there is one book in the whole of Oriental literature which should be read above all others, it is in my opinion Lao Tzu's *Book of Tao.* . . . It is one of the profoundest books in the world's philosophy—profound and clear, mystic and practical."

I often feel that the many spawning contemporary mystic cults would do well to stop their fumbling approaches around the edges of such profound wisdom as is found in Tao. For through it all is the integrating principle of the whole, the spirit of a universe that flows as easily and purposefully as a river runs down hill.

I have been a reader of Lao Tzu and his way of life for many years, and carried his poems with me to read at night or when windbound during a canoe trip. He has a feeling of poise, serenity, and complete assurance that lulls me to rest as surely as the sound of a breeze through the trees.

Witter Bynner writes in his book on Lao Tzu, "He was by no means the solitary, unneighborly hermit, or the occult with meditation. Lao Tzu fused mysticism into a philosophy as realistic and down-to-earth as Confucius, but sweetened by the natural and sufficient intuition of rightness with which he believed all men to be endowed."

As a Buddhist, Lao Tzu's philosophy anticipated and contained the humanitarian philosophies that have followed his

—the fundamental expression of heart and mind serving the common good. It is a fair guess no known religion would have found anything unacceptable in his thoughts. As he said in one of his poems, "My way is so simple to feel, so easy to apply, that only a few will feel or apply it." As we survey great thinkers of this world, the contemplators and meditators, poets and philosophers, and how well they mesh together in their panacea of simplicity, we know he was right.

It is comforting to know there is a path followed by minds greater than mine who have blazed paths and portages across the mysterious and unknown to guide simple minds through the maze.

Dr. Albert Einstein says it well: "The most beautiful experience we can have is the mysterious. It is the fundamental emotion which stands at the cradle of true art and true science. Whoever does not know it and can no longer wonder, no longer marvel, is as good as dead and his eyes are dimmed. It was the experience . . . of mystery, even if mixed with fear—that engendered religion. . . . I am satisfied with the mystery of the eternity of life and with the awareness and a glimpse of the marvelous structure of the existing world, together with the devoted striving to comprehend a portion, be it ever so tiny, of the Reason that manifests itself in nature."

It is hard to imagine a mind such as his finding difficulty with meditation, or having to go through elaborate rituals and stage settings to rid his thoughts of what constantly dominated them. Asleep or awake, his mind was never still, for he lived so intensely and completely in the universe he tried to explain that in its truest and broadest sense it was as natural with him as breathing. Constantly in touch with the primal, as he says, "of the existence of something we cannot penetrate, our perceptions of the profoundest reason and the most radiant beauty which only in their most primitive forms are accessible to our minds—it is this knowledge and emotion which constitute true religiosity."

Thus it is with all great minds who feel so close to the eternal mysteries they are part of them. There is no need for them to explain or search and sweep their minds clear as lesser ones have to do. Such minds are always in a contemplative mood of prayer and adoration. Walt Whitman, in his *Leaves of Grass*, said the little that was good was steadily hastening toward immortality, while the evil would merge itself and become lost and dead.

These men wrote of good and evil, simplicity and complexity. Very few spoke of controlled meditation, because their lives were spent in contemplating the good and beautiful. This is what I choose to believe, and as I continue in my explorations of the wilderness and all its wonders, the clamor of a disturbed outside world becomes a slow hum far in the distance.

If I listen carefully from my cabin, I can hear a hum coming from a highway miles to the south. The wind must be right to catch it, and the waters still. I know that out there trucks and automobiles speed toward a destination, carrying produce or people to the land of lakes and woods, possibly to find what I am finding. I trust those who take off in canoes will become part of the great simplicity and beauties around them, will free themselves from the shackles of personal wishes and desires and attain a humble attitude of mind. I hope their success in fishing, miles to be covered, or pictures taken will be only a small part of their real experience, so they can know the peace and fulfillment of Tao as interpreted by Lao Tzu.

IMMORTALITY

The world of nature does no violence to faiths that speak of personal immortality or reincarnation, for a basic truth encompasses them both.

Since his earliest beginnings, man has dreamed of Valhallas, of heavens with pearly gates, happy hunting grounds, and Nirvanas, places somewhere in the far beyond where troubles, suffering, hunger, fear, and oppression would be over. Legions have died in battle with the assurance their reward was waiting for them in a haven of the blessed. Man has believed when he died it was not the end, but he would live on in another world in the dark unknown void of space.

Most religious faiths speak of a resurrection in which all will come to judgment, to be consigned, if found worthy, to a heaven of unbelievable bliss and beauty, or, if evil and accursed, to the fires of an eternal hell. When this concept arose in the human mind we do not know, but excavations of caves and burial sites of Stone-Age men of thirty to fifty thousand years ago, and possibly long before that, have unearthed evidence of its presence in the custom of surrounding the dead with food and other things needed in the afterlife. Today the vast majority of the human race believes firmly in a hereafter in which the body will be reconstituted, where all will be young and happy once more. Few realize the real immortality is of the mind and spirit.

I am no final authority, but, being a naturalist acquainted with the phenomena of birth, death, and the progressions of change in all forms of life, it seems logical for modern man in his profound knowledge to accept the inevitable: that all creatures, including man, are born to live an allotted span. The world of nature does no violence to faiths that speak of personal immortality or reincarnation, a basic truth encompasses them both.

I am satisfied with a simpler solution, which brings more comfort and peace to me than old beliefs no matter how revered and ancient their origins may be: the memories of those I cannot forget, the joy they have given, and the impact they have had. Certainly they are gone physically and "dust to dust" is no empty phrase, but the real truth in what they were and did lives on, each person leaving his own evidence of his time on earth. It is like a stone thrown into a calm pool, its ripples spreading wider and wider, possibly into infinity.

We can give innumerable examples of great minds who, over the ages, have left their imprint on mankind, but I wish to choose only a few, woodsmen, friends, and co-workers who illustrate what I mean, those who in some way have left an indelible impression on me and my work, touching many more through my writings and other activities—ripples in the pool of life, which never stop. Did not someone say: "He who disturbs a flower may disturb a star"?

I have just returned from Alaska and have vivid memories not only of the modern oil boom but of the days of the gold rush of 1898. Whenever I think of Alaska—and I know it well—I realize it is Robert Service who had the most influence on me. Somehow in his poems he caught the spirit of the North, the cold, suffering, and hardship in pursuit of some bonanza. His little cabin is still at Dawson, near the mouth of the fabulous Klondike where it flows into the Yukon, and now is a shrine to thousands. He made no fortune there, but left a feeling for the land and captured its lure as no other man has ever done.

Even modern migrants streaming there today—dreaming, as their forebears did three-quarters of a century ago, of making a killing in the new riches of oil along the Arctic coast—feel the same about Service. Old Alaskans still quote him, and the new breed, too, the roustabouts, the old drillers, the truck and bulldozer operators, the engineers, flyers, cooks, and maintenance men surging north by the thousands. In the Great Land he will never be forgotten; he spoke for them all of this harsh and beautiful land where everything is on such a vast and titanic scale it dwarfs all they have ever seen.

I have listened to grizzled old-timers quote him unashamedly with a misty look in their eyes.

"There's a whisper in the night wind,
    there's a star agleam to guide us,
And the wild is calling, calling—let us go."

~~~~~~

"Have you gazed on naked grandeur
    where there's nothing else to gaze on?"

~~~~~~

"In the hush of mountain vastness,
    in the flush of midnight skies,
I am the land that listens, I am the land that broods."

~~~~~~

"I've stood in some mighty-mouthed hollow
That's plumb full of hush to the brim . . ."

Some call them crude unlettered doggerel and perhaps
they are right, but he touches the hearts of men and for that he
will live on as long as Alaskan wilderness remains.
My maternal grandmother made an impression on me
more deeply perhaps than anyone else during my childhood.
She alone understood what was within me, a waif of the
wilds, and between us was a precious pact of mystery and love
as vivid today as when I was a boy. She was a gentle soul who
loved the out-of-doors, and I felt a closeness to her that has
never diminished. It was she who used to get up early in the
morning when I wanted to go brook-trout fishing. We would
have breakfast together and talk about trout, where I was
going, and the great adventures I might have. I shall never
forget the look in her eyes of complete oneness, and when I
fished some stream each trout I caught was for her. It was she
who always waited for me, and when it was dusk before I
found my way home, there was always a light in the window
and I knew what was ahead. In my book *The Singing Wilderness,* I devoted a chapter to her and I should like to quote the
final paragraph:

" 'Look, Grandma,' I say, opening the lid of my creel. She
sniffs the wild sweet smell of trout fresh from the creek, and
I tell her the story of each one, the shining dark one with
spots glowing like rubies, the two ten-inchers from under the
bank. Her eyes are full of wonderment as we go over the
stream, pool by pool, rapids by rapids, listening to the birds,
seeing the flowers, hearing the water, and when I tell her of
the big one I lost, she suffers with me.
"Then under the light of the kitchen lamp at a table spread

with a clean checkered cloth, we sit down to a feast of trout, milk and fresh bread, an eighty-year-old lady and a boy of ten, to talk of robins and spring and the eternal joy of fishing."

Walt Hurn, a Canadian Ranger of the old school whose cabin was on King's Point in the Quetico, was unschooled in the ways of the outside world, but he left me with a different feeling for a way of life he epitomized. I looked forward during my guiding days to stopping with him whenever I could, just to sense something unexplainable that was always there, a certain indefinable feeling of belonging, integrity, and lack of emotion. My memories are many, but one stands out as clearly today as it did fifty years ago. I came in around the Point and watched him trolling for a pike just out from the cabin. It was almost dusk and he did not know I was there and I did not speak. It was utterly calm at that moment and he was part of the silence. When he finally turned and came in, he was not surprised or effusive, merely raised his hand in greeting as he beached the canoe.

Jack Linklater, half Scotch and half Cree, was one of the finest woodsmen in the North and just being with him gave me a sense of identity with the past, of Indians and fur traders, mystery and understanding of things most others did not know. At times he heard wilderness music and was amazed I did not hear it as clearly as he. What he heard I do not know, and can only guess. When he drowned on Jackfish Bay, I felt bereft, for his kind is mostly gone now, but I shall always remember, for he forged a link between me and a nebulous background I had not been aware of.

Wallace Atwood from Yale and Clark University, a renowned geologist with whom I made a glaciological survey, made me feel a sense of the immensity of time and space of the glacial periods. When he said to me, "The ice in the great continental glacier was moving forward as a huge rock-shod rasp, scraping off the soils, subsoils, and solid rock, changing the courses of rivers, gouging out lakes, smoothing the bases of the old Laurentian Mountains to a level plateau," I got a continental grasp I did not have before. Never again would I see grooves in the rocks, a glacial esker, or potholes in an ancient riverbed in the same way, for now those glaciers lived.

A. R. Cahn was one of the first ecologists, and after spending three months with him cruising over the Quetico-Superior and far beyond, I became imbued with the broader concept of ecology, that nothing stands alone and is closely allied to everything else. I knew at last the howl of a wolf can be as strange and unfathomable as the mysteries of a swamp, forest, or lake in the pattern of life, but what he really gave me was an ecological perspective that molded my thinking.

J. E. Potzger, paleobotanist of Butler University, taught me to see the "phantom forests" of the past by the simple method of drilling down to the bottom of glacial bogs and identifying the indestructible pollen grains still intact in muck deposited thousands of years before. "Phantom forests" he called them, and today when I see a bog, I remember once the pollen from trees no longer present, drifted onto the open water and settled there into the decaying vegetation,

Herman DeCosta was a Buddhist, the first I had known, who became a close friend of mine. Writer, philosopher, and teacher, we made many trips together and it was through him I learned what Buddhism meant. Though I had read about its meanings, it was different living with someone who actually practiced the faith. Once I asked him to tell what its basic tenets were, and he replied, "Humbleness before God and nature, selflessness and tolerance in a world of bigotry and greed, simplicity in one of complexity." He opened doors to a vision of a way of life billions of others follow.

C. K. Leith, head of the University of Wisconsin's geology department and a professor of mine, talked of floating continents, of a fluid magma underneath, of great land masses tearing themselves away from each other, and the earth's surface floating and viscous. Now when I hear of the probing of ocean depths and finding gigantic rifts in the undersea surfaces, of continental tectonic plates pushing against each other, creating such enormous and unstable areas as the San Andreas fault along the West coast of this continent, I know he was half a century before his time. He contributed to my grasp of earth processes, and all who knew him had their horizons so broadened they could never go back to narrowness in their views.

Blair Fraser, writer and famous commentator on world events, died running the Rollway Rapids on the Petawawa River north of Algonquin. One of my beloved voyageurs on many expeditions in the Far North, Blair went the way he wanted to go, with the sound of white water in his ears. Sir Wilfred Laurier wrote of the land we traveled: "The treasures of the Canadian shield have been won in the end because a certain kind of man has always been drawn to this harsh grey land."

In an article I wrote for the *Beaver* after Blair's death I said, "Blair was indeed that 'certain kind of man' in his devotion to the North, and I believe he had absorbed some of its strength and unyielding hardness now needed in a world questioning old verities and convictions." What did Blair give me? It was an identification with his feeling for the North, and our own as well, a strengthening perhaps of the sense of its real value.

I have a painting before me by A. Y. Jackson, one of the Immortal Seven of Canada, who more than any other group of artists caught the harsh reality and beauty of the Canadian shield. This late autumn painting, "Snowstorm Over Algoma," shows the fading color with snow softly drifting down, a few blackened stubs with a wisp of smoke rising above them in the foreground, snow that would soon extinguish the fire. The last time I met Jackson was at Great Bear where he had gone to catch the fall glory of the tundra once more. He was eighty then, but as alive and excited about the prospect as though he were still young. What did he also give me? What did the whole group of the Immortal Seven give me? A sense of glory, space, and hard magnificence, which will live in the hearts and minds of Canadians forever.

Such personalities—and they are only a few of the many who have influenced my way of thinking—represent the kind of immortality I can comprehend. Their impact on the world and those fortunate enough to have known them is incalculable. They made great ripples in their time, ripples that will never cease moving.

THE EMERGENT GOD

~~~~~~~~~~~~~~~~~~~~~~~~~~~
~~~~~~~~~~~~~~~~~~~~~~~~~~~

,he saying in the scriptures
the Kingdom of God is within you"
has any credence, the new emergence of its true meaning
becomes one of ultimate and conclusive simplicity,
with God the symbol of a broader
and more beautiful concept.

An emergent God is to some a preposterous supposition, a heresy, but more and more people are pondering this greatest of all questions than ever before. In this age of inquiry into the verities of faith, morals, and ethics, the old acceptance of a historic God figure is being interpreted today in a far more comprehensive and intelligent way than it has been in the past. It is not the doubt of the existence of God; everyone knows there is a power beyond the comprehension of man, a God above all, the very essence of existence and belief.

The concept of a new understanding is not a fallacy, nor is it a breaking away from ancient convictions, but rather a change in conception, one based on the explosion of knowledge of the world, the entire universe, and the mind of man. I know no more than anyone else what the final outcome will be, but I am convinced out of the probing and conjecturing

may come a vision which will mean much to the happiness and fulfillment of the dreams and hopes of men.

Coleridge stated that the human imagination inherits and continues the divine activity of Logos, the Word, as well as the common origin of language and consciousness; and that man's creative imagination can be applied not only to the contemplation of God but to nature herself.

What are we saying today? We are saying the eternal element is the soul and spirit of man, a non-material power of reason and logic that dominates the direction of the cosmos and the world we know. If the saying in the scriptures "the Kingdom of God is within you" has any credence, the new emergence becomes one of ultimate and conclusive simplicity, with God the symbol of a broader and more beautiful concept understandable to millions. When He is symbolical in everything, then divinity is the highest goal of existence. It is not so much the contemplation of God as the creation of an ideal consummation.

What, we may ask, is meant by the ideal consummation? It is living in unity with the great goal, not only individual spiritual unison, but one for the greater good of all mankind. If the divine spark is within us all, the thing to worship is man's capacity for love, beauty, awareness, and good. There is something that cannot be measured: the miracle by which man evolved out of matter and developed his mind.

The old idols and fetishes are being abandoned, for the new idea is based no longer on ignorance, blind faith, or intuition, but on knowledge and reason, with the major premise uppermost that spiritual development is all-important and our great goal is to seek godliness in our lives. Nature is a gift of God and a blossom more wonderful than the most ingenious of our machines. A civilization with no love of nature or appreciation of its true meaning as a symbol of God is doomed to primeval barbarism.

René Dubos in his latest book, *God Within*, says the title is a direct translation from the Greek *entheos,* from which the word "enthusiasm" is derived, a form of subconscious inspiration formalizing the forces that create private worlds out of the cosmos and enable life to express itself in countless individuals and ways of thinking.

"Places, rather than geographical sites, evoke life situations, appear to possess a transcendental quality and a rich diversity of persons and cultures, are an expression with each member of the human species incarnating the spirit and genius of the place in which he developed. The biological truth," he says, "is so complex it defies scientific statement. No landscape reveals its full potential until it has been given its myth by love, works, and the art of man. Genius of Place is the living relationship between a particular location and the people who derive from it and add to it the aspects of humanness. There is more to the uniqueness of a place than topography and climate, genetics, economics, or the politics of its population. It is an integral part of the organic form of man."

The Quetico-Superior country takes on new meaning for me through Dubos's insight. It is far more than an area, more than rocks, lakes, and forests I have written about. It has a genius all its own, for it incarnates all the various meanings within me and those who have come to love and appreciate it for what it really is. To all it has a certain quality embodied in the myths we know, through the work we have done and the art and imaginations of those it has affected.

Le Compt du Nouy, speaking of religions, says, "They are opposed to one another in their form, in the material details of the cult, and in the human interpretation of symbols.

They all agree on the existence of God, on the virtues, and moral rules. Purity, goodness, beauty, and faith are venerated everywhere and it is they which should rule."

Religion is not a question of form but the interpretation of symbols and recognition of certain basic principles. They all trend toward the ultimate goal of maturing personality, a humanness that can flower into a fuller and more perfect state of comprehension. If "God is within us," this is exactly what it means, the development of soul and spirit, and within the context of emergence lies the answer to our constant search.

Thoreau said, "The human soul is the silent harp in God's quire, whose strings need only be swept by the divine breath to chime in with the harmonies of creation." He would agree with the old definition of grace, that it is the outward expression of the inward harmony of the soul.

One can read the highest and innermost thoughts of brilliant and profound minds, and they all seem to be saying the same thing: that God is man's greatest symbol and striving toward Him his highest aspiration. If this is the true meaning of the growing emergence of a new concept of God, the entire world will be the better for it.

"I cannot believe that God plays dice with the Cosmos," said Einstein, and long before that Spinoza declared, "The greatest good of the mind is the knowledge of God." Both died before there was much talk about an emerging God, but I am confident in the depths of their mutual understanding, they would have endorsed the concept, as well as the statement from the New Testament that "God is love and he that dwelleth in love dwelleth in God."

Wise men over the ages have not spoken of the emerging God but in their wisdom have anticipated Him. Perhaps the time has come when man, owing to his great knowledge, will find the God he has been looking for, a God who is in no sense a violation of ancient questioning or the conclusions of those who have lived and struggled with their doubts only to come out with much the same assertions we are beginning to accept today.

For centuries, the searching has gone on for a God who is simple and understandable, one who can be incorporated into our lives naturally. How much better to feel the presence of godliness around and within us than to conjecture vainly as to exactly what form He should take. We shall never really know what God is, any more than the meaning of the Word.

Man's only goal, that of human destiny, is the evolution of his mind to the point where he, and mankind as a whole, becomes aware of love, beauty, and truth. This is the emergent God, and if man works toward it constantly in his outlook, thoughts, and actions, he may become Godlike.

The great theologian Abraham Heschel said, "The nature of God is that man should have ends, not only needs . . . therefore the deepest passion in any real human person is a craving for the meaning of existence. . . . God is the meaning beyond absurdity."

Beyond absurdity has tremendous meaning, because it challenges the empty suppositions of those who have failed to find satisfying answers. No naturalist, theologian, or philosopher can tolerate a statement that infers we are still only matter, that there is no logic, reason, or power behind the miracles we have discovered in the boundless universe. Such a statement denies the intuitive perceptions of countless great minds and nullifies everything of meaning in our culture that has been striven for since the beginning.

How much better to assent to the idea of a new dynamic concept regarding the gift of life, embracing the God of our fathers with an interpretation that makes it a living part of existence, than to continue accepting the mythical visions of old. This to me is the essence of religion, knowing the presence of God, the emergent God, who sooner or later will be accepted by all.

I like what the great historian Will Durant concludes in his *Lessons of History:* "The past is not merely a warning reminder of man's crimes and follies, but also an encouraging remembrance of generative souls—a celestial city, a spacious country of the mind, wherein a thousand saints, statesmen, scientists, poets, artists, musicians, lovers, and philosophers still live, speak, teach, carve, and sing.

"The historian will not mourn because he can see no meaning in human existence except what man puts into it. Let it be our pride that we may put meaning into our lives and sometimes a significance that transcends death."

EPILOGUE

*Only when we look at the earth
as civilized thinking men with enlightened insight
will the full measure of human evolution
be possible. We must know the values
which once sustained us are still there
in those parts of the world we have not ravished.*

Not long ago, on a clear sunny day, I flew across the continent from New York to San Francisco and pictured the land as it was at the time of discovery: beautiful, verdant, and untouched. Whales were spouting off Nantucket, the timber stood tall and dark along the coastal flats. There were salmon and shad in rivers running clean and full to the sea.

We passed high over the blue misty ridges of the Appalachians, which pinned the first colonists to their beachheads. Deer and elk were everywhere then and clouds of wildfowl darkened the sky. We flew across the checkerboard pattern of farms over the valley of the Ohio, but all I saw was the old primeval forest of green extending unbroken to the Mississippi.

Beyond the great river were endless grassy plains where millions of buffalo roamed. Rising foothills appeared, then the snow-covered peaks of the Rockies, with the broad expanse of the painted deserts beyond, and finally the ramparts of the coastal Sierras, the dark border of the sequoias, and the crashing white surf of the blue Pacific.

Now all of that was changed, and as I fastened my seat belt, I wondered how much further we would go in the final subjection of the America I had imagined during the flight, if urban sprawl, growing industry, and population would increase to the point where freedom and the old dream would be lost.

The ultimate question is what kind of world we really want: more of endless exploitation or one involving a proper relationship with our land? Would we choose wisely in the crucial years ahead?

As I drove into the great romantic city of San Francisco, I did not see the traffic or hear the clamor, but wondered more about the purpose of man and what actually constitutes the good society; and I was cheered because of the realization of the emerging truth that we are no longer omnipotent.

I also knew while science could redress the wrongs we have inflicted, it would not be the answer unless our spiritual welfare was the overriding consideration and our search for utopia reflected fundamental human needs. If we could embrace this concept and become part of the order and reason that govern existence, we would be acting with wisdom. If we could grasp even an intimation of what is meant by the imponderables, we would know what the sages have been telling us for centuries: that our goal should be wholeness in the minds of men.

The great challenge is to build a base of knowledge and understanding of such depth, clarity, and power that it cannot be ignored, and never forget that the stature of man and the development of his culture has increased because of beauty, mystery, and vision, not through ugliness, warped and twisted psychosis. Only when we know what a balanced ecology really means can we live in harmony; only when we know intuitively that such values are more important than all others will we restore our flagging spirits.

Juan Ramón Jiménez, winner of the Nobel Prize for Literature in 1956, said: "When a man can live tranquilly in the out-of-doors without fear of anything on earth or in space, not because he is a savage, but because he is thoroughly civilized, he has arrived through himself at the ultimate, that is to say the primal, having rid himself of all that is useless and unserviceable. This return to the primal is the ultimate to which a man can attain; it can make him complete master of himself, absolute friend to others, a poet without needing to write or without an academy."

Only when we look at the earth as civilized thinking men with enlightened insight will the full measure of human evolution be possible. Man's problem is far more than escape from his predicament; he must know the reasons for his discontent and, in spite of having been torn from his old environment, realize the values which once sustained him are still there in those parts of the world he has not ravished.

One of the most vital tasks of modern man is to bridge the enormous gap between his old way of life and his growing vision of the new. Though man will always cherish his memory of the frontiers and be proud of the courage and fortitude of his pioneer ancestors, he is now aware of the vast extent of his knowledge. If he can span the past and the present and look at the land for the first time as a truly civilized man, then, and only then, will he know his full potential. If he can move into the future and live in the coming world with the ancient dreams that always stirred him, and merge them with the new, he can approach the era ahead with hope.

With our vast knowledge we are hounded by doubt. Just the fact the smallest structures of matter with their neutrons and protons move with the same precision and order as the galaxies, that solar systems are dying and being born again, makes us wonder and question the purpose of all we have learned. We also know there are certain things that cannot be measured scientifically, secrets that defy rational deduction, with no answer to the concepts of love, imagination, or the flowering of man's mind. Let us never succumb to the doctrine of despair and absurdity, for this would be man's last pitiful cry for meaning: if he accepts it he is lost.

As I conclude these reminiscences of my life in the wilderness and look forward to new travels down other waterways, I do as I have always done in the past, a woodsman's ritual when leaving any campsite: look around to see if there is anything left, forgotten, or undone, perhaps listen for a moment to some melody I sensed there, and may hear again along the trail.

I know the music will be new and different in the years ahead, for with the immense research programs going on in an infinite variety of diverse fields of inquiry all over the world, we are going to make discoveries of such magnitude and significance they are bound to change our outlook and beliefs, our life-styles, priorities, and objectives in a way no one can even remotely predict. We may well discover life on other planets and learn to communicate with intelligences we do not now comprehend, which will expand human minds into undreamed realms of consciousness, but with all this the wilderness has taught me eternal values will never change.

Sigurd F. Olson (1899–1982) was one of the greatest environmentalists of the twentieth century. A conservation activist and popular writer, Olson introduced a generation of Americans to the importance of wilderness. He served as president of the Wilderness Society and the National Parks Association, and as a consultant to the federal government on wilderness preservation and ecological problems. He earned many honors, including the highest possible from the Sierra Club, National Wildlife Federation, and Izaak Walton League.

Olson's books include *The Singing Wilderness* (1956), *Listening Point* (1958), *The Lonely Land* (1961), *Runes of the North* (1963), *Open Horizons* (1969), *The Hidden Forest* (1969), *Wilderness Days* (1972), *Reflections from the North Country* (1976), and *Of Time and Place* (1982). His books created a new genre of nature writing that was infused with beauty and respect for our nation's wild places. He was a recipient of the John Burroughs Medal, the highest honor in nature writing, and his books frequently appeared on best-seller lists across the nation.

For most of his life, Olson lived and worked in Ely, Minnesota, gateway to the Quetico-Superior region.